Maximising Tax-Free Business Expenses

THE COMPLEMENTARY WEBSITE

The http://books.indicator.co.uk website gives you instant access to all the ready-to-use documents, tools, policies, etc. that complement this publication.

Go to

http://books.indicator.co.uk

and enter your access code
XXR393

THE CD-ROM

Don't have access to the Internet?
Call Customer Services on 01233 653500 to request a CD-ROM.

indicator

ISBN 978-1-906892-34-0

First Edition - Third print - E01P3

Cover: ©iStockphoto.com

Introduction

Putting expenses through your business will save you money, but how much will the Taxman allow you to get away with? Remember, he only ever gives you his biased interpretation.

With this book you'll be able to pick up suggestions and valuable tips on how to keep more of your money for yourself and away from the Taxman's grasp. It sets out, clearly and in one place, the ground rules for legitimately putting expenses through your business. You'll be able to see how much you could save by putting an expense through your company rather than paying for it yourself.

Most people picking up this book will just want to "get the paperwork right" when dealing with the Taxman. Others, however, would like to take a more determined approach to legitimately claiming all that they can, but at the same time aren't sure where to start. With this in mind, we have divided the book into two parts.

Section 1 deals with the expense claims themselves and Section 2 sets out the times that you might wish your company to pay on your behalf as part of a planned addition to your remuneration package. You'll be able to pick up new ideas that you may not have otherwise thought of, plus there's advice on how to implement them.

Whichever section takes your immediate interest, your objectives should be the same: how to make sure that you're not taxed personally and that your company can claim a deduction for the expenditure against its own Corporation Tax bill.

April 2011

Table of contents

Section 1 - Expense claims

Chapter 1 - Why claim expenses?

Chapter 2 - Claiming through your company

Chapter 3 - Scrutiny from the Taxman

Chapter 4 - Your expenses claim

Chapter 5 - Your company's expenses policy

Chapter 6 - Current dispensation process

Chapter 7 - Mileage allowance

Chapter 8 - Other motoring expenses

Chapter 9 - UK fares and travel

Chapter 10 - UK subsistence

Chapter 11 - Overseas travel and subsistence

Chapter 12 - Hotels and other accommodation

Chapter 13 - Telephones

Chapter 14 - Entertaining

Chapter 15 - Computer consumables

Chapter 16 - Working from home

Chapter 17 - Miscellaneous expenses

Chapter 18 - Cash advances

Chapter 19 - Maximising VAT recovery

© Maximising Tax-Free Business Expenses, Indicator

Section 2 - Further angles and ideas

Chapter 20 - Company tax deduction

Chapter 21 - Use of home by a company

Chapter 22 - Garden maintenance

Chapter 23 - Gifts

Chapter 24 - Language lessons

Chapter 25 - Magazine subscriptions

Chapter 26 - Paying for a holiday

Chapter 27 - Private tutors

Chapter 28 - School fees

Chapter 29 - Personal trainers

Chapter 30 - Cars for the family

Chapter 31 - Company plane (or yacht)

Chapter 32 - Gym membership

Chapter 33 - Garage storage

Chapter 34 - Nannies

Chapter 35 - The weekend away

Chapter 36 - Domestic help

Chapter 37 - Use of the company villa

Chapter 38 - Advisors' fees

Chapter 39 - Parking near work

Chapter 40 - Computer equipment

Technical notes

Appendices

SECTION 1

Expense claims

CHAPTER 1

Why claim expenses?

1.1. PUTTING EXPENSES THROUGH YOUR BUSINESS

Ask any entrepreneur and they'll tell you that their primary motivation for setting up in business is to make a profit. In fact, the profit motive is one of the tests used by the Taxman to determine whether an activity can be genuinely classed as a "trade" as opposed to an "investment" activity.

Profit is generated by the maximisation of sales revenues and the minimisation of costs. Unfortunately, for almost every pound earned in profit there will be taxes to pay in one form or another, and whilst the majority of us accept that taxation is inevitable we also want to keep our liabilities to a minimum.

One way to do this is to simply earn less profit in the first place, but this defeats the object of going in to business; nobody sets out to be unsuccessful. But it is possible to reduce taxable profits by increasing your tax deductible expenses. You could achieve this by finding new ways to spend your money, maybe renting flash offices or holding lavish parties for your customers. Maybe you could charter a yacht for your next business meeting?

We can all think of ways to spend money. An office suite with an upmarket address makes good business sense if it will attract more and better business. However, if you can take some of your day-to-day "personal expenditure" and convert it into "business expenditure" that can be charged against tax, you can achieve your goal of reducing your taxes and keeping more of the profit for yourself.

1.2. CAN YOU CHARGE EVERYTHING TO YOUR COMPANY?

In an ideal scenario we would charge every penny we spend against the business and pay no taxes at all, but this is obviously unrealistic. The Taxman may be a lot of things, but he isn't a fool. After all, if you were to consistently show losses on your tax returns but lived a privileged lifestyle, then before you could say "Lester Piggott" he'd start making a few enquiries!

The reality is that for most owner-managers the line between their private and business lives is so blurred that you can't always tell where one ends and the other begins. With some things it's more obvious than others, like the company car for example, which clearly has both business and personal uses. Others are not so straightforward. For example, how many people take work home with them? If the accounts are done on the kitchen table, is the cost of heating and lighting that room attributable to business or private use? What about telephone calls, or using the Internet for research? How many people pick up bits and pieces for the office along with the groceries? Does that make it a business trip? And that newspaper you read every morning with the business section...?

1

The list could go on, but the point is clear: there are times when what we naturally think of as household expenses also have a work-related element to them. These can, in part or in whole, be quite legitimately charged against profit.

But don't be fooled into thinking you can take liberties with the tax rules. There are clear principles that have to be followed for the expense claim to be considered legitimate by the Taxman. A quick review of the rules will demonstrate why.

1.3. HOW MUCH CAN YOU SAVE?

The question many people will be asking at this stage is whether the amount saved in tax will be worth the extra hassle of making the claim, particularly for those of us who aren't over keen on paperwork.

EXAMPLE

Imagine you can turn £50 per month into business expenses. That's £600 per year, and at a tax rate of 20%, this will save your company £120 in Corporation Tax. And that's not all, because you have just saved the company the equivalent in, say, salary costs for you of £600 net of tax. The tax and NI bill on the gross equivalent of £1,034 is £434 for you and another £143 for the company, making £697 saved all together. Now it starts to look like a good proposition!

1.4. THE TAX RULES

1.4.1. Rule 1 - Incorporated businesses

The rules for limited companies follow the same principles as those for unincorporated businesses. Here, however, there is a fundamental difference: with sole traders and partnerships there is no distinction in law between the business and the person or people operating that business.

With a limited company comes the "veil of incorporation", which has been used to describe the separation between the business owners (the shareholders) and the company itself. In the eyes of the law they are two separate entities.

What this means is that expenses invoiced to the company belong to the company itself and can be properly charged to the company. They do not belong to the directors who are running the company or the shareholders who own it.

Note. You can't just charge all your household expenses to the company because of the "wholly and exclusively" rule.

1.4.2.   Rule 2 - Benefits-in-kind

Any private element of a business expense is taxed on the employee under the benefits-in-kind system.

The most common examples are the free use of company cars and the provision of fuel, private medical insurance, and the payment of fees or subscriptions. Each year the employer will enter the value of the benefits on Form P11D and the employee will pay tax on those benefits, usually through an adjustment to their PAYE code.

1.4.3.   Rule 3 - Employees

The third point is an extension of the "wholly and exclusively" rule and is applicable to employees, which of course includes company directors. The claimed expenditure must be "wholly, exclusively and necessarily incurred in the performance of the duties of the employment". Basically, if it's not necessary for the employee to incur the expense, then it can't be claimed.

This may, at first glance, look like a killer blow for anyone wanting to make a more "inventive" claim. Fortunately for us however, a company director's prime duty, as enshrined in company law, is to act in the best interests of the shareholders, i.e. to make a profit on their behalf. Therefore, any expenditure incurred to this end is a legitimate expense of the company. It will need to be demonstrated that this is the case should the Taxman make a challenge, but the point can be argued. Incur the expense for the business, even if there is an incidental private element, and it can properly be claimed.

1.4.4.   Rule 4 - Dispensations

More good news for the employee/director is that there are times when a benefit does not need to be included on the P11D. This is when the Taxman gives a dispensation. This is basically an agreement that certain benefits do not need to be included on the P11D. He will only do this if he is satisfied that there will be no tax payable on the benefit.

An example of this is when an employee is paid travelling expenses. Strictly speaking these should normally be included on the P11D and then claimed back by the individual on their tax return. The net effect is that the benefit is cancelled out by the claim and everyone is happy. The dispensation means that there's no P11D for the company to fill in, and less paperwork for the Taxman to process.

Why claim expenses?

KEY POINTS

- reduce taxable profits by converting some of your day-to-day personal expenditure into tax-deductible business expenses
- it doesn't matter that your accounting profit goes down; it's your spending power that counts
- the expenses have to be "wholly and exclusively" for the purposes of the trade: the expenditure must have been incurred because of your business
- an expense invoiced to the company is payable by the company; any private element is taxed as a benefit-in-kind
- expenses claimed by an employee have to be "wholly, exclusively and necessarily incurred in the performance of their duties"
- take advantage of the grey areas to get your tax bills reduced.

CHAPTER 2

Claiming through your company

2.1. HOW DO YOU CLAIM AS AN EMPLOYEE?

A company director is usually an employee of their company and therefore subject to the strict rules applied to earnings from employment. There are three ways by which an employee can obtain tax relief for expenses incurred on company business.

2.1.1. Claiming on your tax return

Any expense which you can incur as an employee can be claimed as a deduction from your earnings by entering the amount as an expense of employment on the employment pages of your personal tax return. This will reduce your taxable income and can often lead to a tax refund.

➤ *Advantages*

- this is a simple and straightforward method with minimal paperwork

- under self-assessment, the claim for deduction may never be challenged, particularly if it's one that's repeated from year to year.

➤ *Disadvantages*

- only the tax deducted is refunded, never the full expense. So if you incur expenses of £100 and pay tax at 40% you will only get £40 back. Similarly, a basic rate taxpayer will receive a refund of £20

- although they can get through unchallenged, this is the exception not the rule, particularly for a new claim. For larger claims, the Taxman will almost certainly ask for further information before allowing them

- the rules for claiming a deduction as an employee, as we saw in Chapter 1, are very strict and have been interpreted very rigidly by the courts (remember the "wholly, exclusively and necessarily" rule)

- there is no deduction in the accounts of the company and therefore no reduction in the company's Corporation Tax liability.

2.1.2. Claiming a reimbursement

This is where the company refunds the full amount of the expense, or in the case of motor expenses, uses the approved mileage rates to make the reimbursement. The mechanics of this are more complicated than the simple process of a claim through your tax return and are best illustrated by way of an example.

Jim, a company director, draws £100 per month (£1,200 p.a.) from his company for entertaining business associates and potential customers. At the end of the tax year the company accountant adds up the receipts and vouchers supplied by Jim which are the actual costs of the entertaining. However, they total only £1,100.

The accountant will now make an entry on Jim's P11D for the year at Section N under the "Entertaining" heading as follows; *"Cost to you £1,200"*, *"Amount made good £1,100"*, *"Taxable Amount £100"*. "Cost to you" means cost to the employer. "Amount made good" is the actual expenditure incurred on company business and "Taxable Amount" is the benefit-in-kind. Jim will now enter £100 in Box 1.23 on the employment pages of his tax return and he will be taxed on this along with the rest of his earnings. However, if Jim had actually spent £1,300, he would normally claim the extra £100 from the company, and the P11D entries are; *"Cost to you £1,300"*, *"Amount made good £1,300"*, *"Taxable payment £0"*.

If Jim didn't claim the additional £100 from the company he would enter the expense on his tax return. However, he would only be entitled to the tax deduction as discussed at 2.1.1. He will effectively be out of pocket by the difference.

➤ *Advantages*

- the full amount of the expense incurred is obtained, not just the tax refund

- the company will often have an expense charged against profit in its accounts and therefore reduce its Corporation Tax liability (**Note.** This is never the case for entertaining customers, etc.)

- if done correctly, this method of completing the entries on Form P11D and then the tax return gives greater legitimacy to the expense claim. There's nothing the Taxman likes more than correct procedures.

➤ *Disadvantages*

- as with claiming on your tax return, the Taxman can still challenge the deduction under the "wholly, exclusively and necessarily" rule, even if every I is dotted and every T crossed

- there's more paperwork to complete: the company (which may well mean you or your accountant) will have to complete the entries on Form P11D in addition to those already being entered on your tax return. The company will need records to back up the entries it makes on the P11D.

2.1.3. Claiming via a dispensation

A dispensation is an agreement with the Taxman that certain expense payments made do not need to be included on the P11D or on the tax return, the only proviso being that they attract a full tax deduction in the hands of the employee.

Note. In a nutshell, the amount being refunded to the employee exactly covers the amount you would be able to claim back on your tax return and therefore the Taxman isn't going to be out of pocket.

➤ *What can be covered?*

The Taxman's website says any type of expenses payments (apart from round sum allowances) and most benefits-in-kind can be covered, including:

- qualifying travel expenses (but not business mileage payments because this is dealt with under special rules)

- entertaining

- subscriptions to professional bodies or learned societies.

- A dispensation can also apply to non-cash vouchers and credit tokens provided to cover expenses.

➤ *What cannot be covered?*

Includes:

- company cars and vans that are taxable

- private medical insurance

- cheap loans.

Conditions

The Taxman will only allow the dispensation if he is sure that:

- no tax would be payable by the employees on expenses paid or benefits provided

- expenses claims are independently checked and authorised within the firm and, where possible, are supported by receipts.

This second condition presents us with a problem where the owner/manager of the business is the sole employee, or if the directors are effectively authorising their own expense claims. However, it's still possible to use the system if the expenses claimed are fully supported by documentation and your accountant regularly reviews a sample of them.

Change in circumstances

Because a dispensation can only cover the circumstances for which it was issued, and the type and amounts of expenses payments and benefits it specifically refers to, the Taxman will need to be informed of any changes for it to remain effective.

The example given on the Taxman's website is a modification of the system for controlling expenses payments or an alteration to the scale rates for expenses.

If the scale rates are amended in line with price changes, then the Taxman will normally agree without asking further questions, but any changes will mean that the dispensation should not be used until the Taxman has renewed his authorisation.

The only time the Taxman will remove his authorisation is when the situation for which the dispensation was given no longer applies. So in effect once the dispensation has been given, you can keep it until you no longer require it.

➤ *Advantages*

- unlike with certain benefits-in-kind, there's no NI due on payments made under a dispensation. This applies to both the company and the employee making the claim

- there are no entries to make on the tax return for the individual or on the P11D for the employer, so cutting down on the paperwork

- the expenses and benefits are not included as part of your tax assessment or PAYE codes.

➤ *Disadvantages*

- the system is really designed for companies with a number of employees all making similar claims for similar expenses. If you're only going to be making one or two claims a year, then you may decide it's not worth it

- getting the Taxman's permission to use the system means that the chances of getting away with any "imaginative" claims are almost always nil.

2.2. HOW CAN YOU CLAIM AS A DIRECTOR/ SHAREHOLDER?

2.2.1. Director's loan account

Being the owner as well as the manager of your business gives you an advantage not available to ordinary employees. This is because, as a general rule, it's you who runs the company and therefore it's you who ultimately decides what expenses the company incurs. As we outlined in Chapter 1, you can rent an upmarket address if you want to; whether it makes good business sense to do so is another matter, but the choice is still yours.

This is where you can use a bit of imagination and achieve what we looked at previously: getting your personal expenditure into the company as business expenses, and you can do this by utilising your director's loan account (DLA).

Note. A DLA typically arises when a company is set up and the shareholders/directors put their own funds into the company as start-up capital. The company now owes this money to the directors and the funds are available to be drawn on as required, subject to the cash being available.

TIP

The DLA can also be used as a mechanism for the introduction of expenses to the company.

EXAMPLE

Taking our example from earlier, Jim, who is a company director, has spent £1,300 of his own money on entertaining business customers. But because all of the company's spare cash is tied up in working capital, Jim decides not to draw the £1,300 from the company just yet. However, because he's spent the money on company business he knows he can add the sum to his DLA and charge the entertaining in the accounts. The £1,300 is now owed to Jim and he can claim it at a later date.

You could just as easily have waived the money; after all the company belongs to you, so it's only like paying yourself back from your own sources, isn't it? Wrong!

EXAMPLE

Let's say we wind things on another year and we're into a new accounting period. The company now has surplus cash and Jim wants to pay himself a bonus so that he can take Mrs Jim on a holiday that, by coincidence, just happens to cost £1,300. As we know, Jim can't just draw the cash from the company bank account without paying tax on the withdrawal. He has three options:

1. Pay himself a bonus under PAYE.
2. Pay himself a dividend.
3. Borrow the money from the company.

Each of the options will give rise to either a company or a personal tax bill, or in the case of Option 3, both. Option 3 also means the money has to be paid back, so we're back where we started.

Let's say Jim goes for Option 2 and the company declares a dividend of £1,300. As a higher rate taxpayer, Jim will have to pay an extra £325 under self-assessment.

To take the concept one step further, let's imagine that Jim pays himself a salary under PAYE and each month he spends exactly what he takes home, with the result that he doesn't have the additional £325 to pay his personal tax bill. The result? He needs to pay himself another bonus from the company.

TIP

By putting an amount through your DLA as an expense you can simply withdraw the cash tax-free.

Claiming through your company

Documentation

As with everything to do with the Taxman, you must have adequate documentation to support your claim. So if it's an entertaining expense this means keeping receipts, bar bills, credit-card vouchers etc. This may seem like a chore but the more evidence you can gather, the stronger your case.

Note. However, there are no special rules to worry about here. The documentation kept in support of your claim forms part of the company's books in the same way as any other expense invoices do. Unlike putting an entry on your tax return or on a P11D, these claims are not separately identifiable from the rest of the company's day-to-day expenses which will eventually appear in the annual accounts.

This doesn't mean they won't ever be queried by the Taxman. They could be picked up and challenged through an enquiry into the company's tax return or on a PAYE control visit. The point is that the Taxman isn't put on notice that these claims are being made which increases their chances of getting "lost" in the accounts.

What can you claim through a DLA?

The simple answer is: anything and everything, so long as it meets the criteria set out in Chapter 1: it must have been "wholly and exclusively" incurred for the purposes of the trade.

Note. The "necessarily" part doesn't apply here because it's an ordinary business expense not an employee expense.

So it's not just entertaining that you can claim for. It could be a "use of home" claim for doing the books on the kitchen table, calculated as a percentage of your household bills, or perhaps a mileage expense using the appropriate statutory rates.

➤ *Advantages*

- it's simple and straightforward with no P11Ds or entries on your tax return to worry about
- you don't have to get prior approval from the Taxman to get the expense reimbursed
- there's no "necessarily" test to comply with
- you always get a full, tax-free reimbursement and it can be drawn as and when required
- the company gets a full deduction as appropriate.

➤ *Disadvantages*

- you must have a certain amount of documentation to support your claim.

2.2.2. The company pays the bill

An invoice issued to the company is a legitimate company expense and is rightly payable by the company. It may not always be allowable for tax purposes or there may be some personal tax to pay because of the "wholly and exclusively" rule, but nevertheless this is one way in which a personal expenditure can become a business expense.

Home phone bill

A common example of this is the company paying the director's home phone bill. This is legitimised on the ground that many owner/managers make business calls in the evenings and at weekends. Added to this element of business use is the convenience of paying the bill on one account along with the office phone, fax, and Internet etc. Any private calls, plus the rental which is always classed as private, are taxed as a benefit-in-kind and will have to be declared on Form P11D.

With something like the company paying a private phone bill it's difficult to tell where the business element starts and the private element finishes. Unlike with, say, a company car, there are no specific rules to follow when calculating the benefit. Strictly speaking, each call should be analysed between business and private, but this is not always practicable and as a result, a "reasonable" percentage is often agreed with the Taxman.

> **TIP**
>
> One important point to remember is that any invoice has to be issued in the name of the company at the company address, not the director at their home address. If this isn't done, then it's treated as being remuneration and the whole bill becomes subject to NI.

Warning. What you can't do is charge expenses falsely to the company; it's one thing having an expense with a private element; it's another thing altogether to have purely personal bills invoiced to the company. This is known as the "pecuniary liability principle", where the employer effectively discharges a debt between the director and a third party, and it will be treated as earnings by the Taxman.

➤ *Advantages*

- the Taxman will often agree the private element on a percentage basis so there's not much record-keeping to do
- a bill in the company's name gives it extra credibility
- there's no having to claim an expense as it's already been paid for you.

➤ *Disadvantages*

- you have to include the private element on a P11D.

2.2.3.   Dispensations from the Taxman

For each director, and all employees earning more than £8,500, you have to complete an annual return of benefits-in-kind and expenses (Form P11D). The completion of these forms can be extremely time consuming. However, this can be made easier, or avoided altogether, by obtaining a dispensation from the Taxman.

A P11D dispensation is an agreement between the Taxman and an employer designed to facilitate easier P11D processing. Once agreed, it permits you to exclude most business expenses, reimbursed or provided to employees, from the P11D. Typically, these include travel and subsistence expenses (e.g. taxi fares, hotel bills), entertaining and professional subscriptions.

Trap. If you fail to submit a return for all expenses and you don't have a dispensation, you could face fines of up to £3,000 per form and an increased risk of your business being selected for a PAYE/NI investigation.

The Taxman is primarily looking for an independent checking system that will ensure that the rules of the dispensation are followed. He may therefore reject a dispensation claim for a director who checks their own expenses.

One-man companies

If yours is a one-man company, your accountant could provide a checking service. Once a year may be sufficient where only a small volume of expenses are incurred.

TIP

You can increase the amount included in a dispensation without applying to HMRC. The Taxman's Employment Income Manual **(EIM30083)** states that *"the amount may be up rated annually by the employer without the need to seek HMRC's agreement, as long as the annual increase is equal to or less than the annual increase in the Retail Prices Index (RPI) for the same period."*

They can be withdrawn

Dispensations can be withdrawn by the Taxman if it appears to him that they are not being correctly administered, e.g. it's being applied to types of expenditure not originally part of the agreement. Indeed, the Taxman announced a couple of years ago that where he considers the terms of a dispensation are not being adhered to, he will revoke it retrospectively. This would mean having to complete Forms P11D for all the previous years affected. Worse still, it could result in additional PAYE and NI liabilities, penalties and interest charges.

TIP

Check the operation of your dispensation each year. To do this you will only need to review a one-in-ten sample of your records to prove that the terms you agreed have been followed correctly. Keep a copy of the checks you make to counter any attempt by the Taxman to later ask for retrospective P11Ds to be submitted.

Expenses policy

In order to a get a reporting dispensation from the Taxman, your procedures for the submission and authorisation of expense claims need to be well documented and communicated to employees.

In addition to the claim form, the Taxman will also ask for a copy of your expenses policy. He will grant a dispensation if he's happy that no tax will be payable by the employees on the expenses or benefits provided. He wants to know that you have a good system in place to ensure that only business expenses are being reimbursed before agreeing to a dispensation. Therefore, our policy covers all the rules and requirements for legitimate claims, such as prior authorisation and provision of VAT receipts. He will also want to see that the expense claims are always authorised by someone other than the claimant.

The Taxman will give you a dispensation if he is satisfied, on the basis of what you tell him, that no additional tax would be payable by the employee concerned on certain expenses payments and benefits. It's important that you let him know if you alter your system for controlling expense payments and benefits, increase their amounts, change their nature or make any other change that might affect their taxability.

Download Zone

For an **Expenses Policy**, visit **http://books.indicator.co.uk**. You'll find the access code on page 2 of this book.

Who can be covered by a dispensation?

- directors, where their expense claims are independently checked by an authorised person, or where full receipts or relevant vouchers are held in support of the expenditure.

- all other employees whose claims are independently checked and authorised by another person, except

  - where the exemptions provided by this dispensation notice and any way would bring their total earnings below £8,500; and

  - there are other payments of expenses and benefits which would thereby cease to be taxable under the benefits code, s.63 of the **Income Tax (Earnings and Pensions) Act 2003**.

Employees not covered by a dispensation

- non-UK domiciled individuals working in the UK who have an employment relationship with an employer resident outside the UK.

2.2.4. Using your company credit card

If you use your company credit card to settle expenses, do you still need to fill in an expenses claim form? The answer is "Yes". Not only does this help support the business justification for such expenditure, it also helps the company identify any VAT included in the expense that it might be able to reclaim from the VATman.

Dispensation

Can company credit cards be covered by a dispensation? Again, the answer is "Yes". The wording from HMRC will be something like:

"This dispensation covers goods or services obtained by means of a company credit/debit card supplied by reason of employment. The employee must reimburse the employer in full for any personal expenses incurred. The cost of any business-related goods or services obtained by the use of the credit card must be in such circumstances that, had the employee incurred it, there would be a deduction for it (under ss.336-338 of the Income Tax (Earnings and Pensions) Act 2003)."

The key point being here that if you do happen to use the company credit card for your own private expenditure, you must reimburse the company in full as soon as possible. Either write it a cheque or get the expense debited to your director's loan account if it has sufficient credit.

Company policy

To give the Taxman the impression that you have this area covered, we would recommend that you add a paragraph about company credit cards to your company's expenses policy. Use something along the lines of:

"Authorised employees who are required to entertain clients regularly on behalf of the Company or otherwise to incur expenses on the Company's behalf will be afforded the facilities for such expenditure, in the form of a credit card. Expenditure will remain subject to the specified Company limits and credit/charge card bills must be supported by receipts."

KEY POINTS

Claiming expenses through your limited company can be done in a variety of ways, and the particular method you use may well vary depending on the nature of the expense. But the most important points to remember are:

- if you claim a deduction on your tax return you can only ever get tax relief at your top rate of tax; never the full amount
- for every pound you can get out of the company you could be saving the equivalent in salary plus the income tax and NI that would have been due under PAYE
- make sure your paperwork is in order so that you can support any claim if there's a challenge. It doesn't just make life easier but gives the Taxman more confidence that the claim is legitimate
- if you pay business expenses to employees or directors, you should consider a P11D dispensation. In our experience many employers either don't apply, or let them expire
- the Taxman will usually agree to simplifying the completion of Forms P11D by using a dispensation, provided that expenses claims are independently checked. A 10% sample of claims must be reviewed each year or your dispensation could be lost when it comes up for renewal.

Claiming through your company

CHAPTER 3

Scrutiny from the Taxman

As with all tax planning you need to be one step ahead of the Taxman. This includes having documentation to hand to take care of the awkward inspector that everybody comes across from time to time.

In truth, the tax rules for deduction of expenses are so strict that they are normally allowed because the Taxman eventually takes a reasonable view. This is very important to know because it will affect the way you approach him. As a general rule, courtesy and a professional approach pay dividends because negotiations will invariably be required over expenses.

Note. The Technical notes also provide a resource for dealing with the Taxman, with relevant case law, useful websites, where to find the official guidance, etc.

3.1. HOW WILL THE TAXMAN KNOW?

With your company's annual self-assessment tax return (CT600) you have to file a full set of accounts, including a detailed profit and loss account. Selecting an expense heading from this, that has perhaps increased dramatically compared to last year, the Taxman may ask for more details/analysis (as an aspect enquiry) thus revealing the costs to the company of a personal expense.

EXAMPLE

If your company can buy medical insurance cover more cheaply than you can, it may make sense for your company to meet this expense. What if your company forgets to put this on your P11D?

If you have booked this cost to say "Insurances" and the Taxman asks for an analysis of this expense heading during an enquiry into your company, he will look for corresponding disclosure of medical insurance on your P11D. If it's not there, your company has submitted an incorrect return and you are into his penalty regime as well as having to pay employers' NI on the figure and interest for late payment.

He will go as far as to send a note to the inspector who deals with your income tax return to say that he thinks it's incomplete too. Oops!

3.2. HOW SHOULD YOU REACT?

How should you handle the Taxman if he comes knocking on your door asking for details about your expenses? In fact, how do you mount a successful defence against the implied suggestion that you might simply be "trying it on"?

Remember, the Taxman doesn't have all the answers. His job is to make sure you're not underpaying your taxes, and he has a big book of rules to help him. But there are also rules in place to see that he plays fair, and there are people looking over his shoulder to make sure he's not wasting time chasing small amounts of tax. If it's seen as uneconomic to pursue an argument, then he will try to reach a compromise. At the end of the day, tax law is full of grey areas and as we have seen it's not always possible to demonstrate clearly where "business" begins and "personal" ends.

There are two golden rules to follow here: **(1)** it's a paper audit. If you've got the documentation right, any argument with the Taxman will be halfway won before you even start; and **(2)** don't be intimidated into backing down without a fight.

3.2.1. Does he always ask the same questions?

The Taxman's procedures during enquiries generally run along the same lines. He will make a list of all the areas he has a problem with and will write to you asking for information. If you have a tax advisor, they will be sent copies of all correspondence. Here are the dos and don'ts in response to this:

- never ignore him. If there are penalties, the rate charged will be reduced if he thinks you've been co-operative. Write a brief letter acknowledging his enquiry and that you will answer in full in due course. This will give you time to prepare your defence

- gather as much information backing up your claim as you can. If you haven't got documentation, write down the facts behind the claim. For example, if you had a trip abroad, you need to demonstrate how it helped your business and that it wasn't just a holiday

- write your reply, responding to each point in turn. Keep to the facts, giving him as much as he needs but no more. Include supporting documentation if you have it

- ask yourself some questions: why is he asking for this? Is he entitled to it? Is it relevant to his enquiry?

- if he has any technical queries, get a tax advisor if you haven't already appointed one.

The Taxman will then consider your response, and either write back for further details or come up with a figure he wants to assess you on.

3.2.2. Will you need to attend an interview?

Generally speaking a meeting with the Taxman is not required, particularly if there are only a small number of queries that are relatively straightforward.

3.3. WHOLLY AND EXCLUSIVELY ATTACK

The Taxman will want to disallow expenses if they are not "wholly and exclusively" for the company's trade.

Let's say you've incurred some expenses partly for business and partly for personal reasons. The rule is that the expenses must be wholly and exclusively incurred for the purposes of the business. This leads to the most important principle, which is duality of purpose. What this means is that if you incur some expense partly for business and partly for other reasons, you don't get part of your expenses allowed - you will get none of them.

EXAMPLE

The best example of a duality of purpose case was that of Miss Anne Mallalieu, a barrister who was obviously able to argue her case with great skill. She still lost. She claimed the expense of buying and keeping clean the black clothing that she was required to wear in court. She did not like the black clothing and wore it only for work. What the Taxman successfully claimed was that she did not only buy the clothes for wearing in court - she had another purpose which was she needed to wear clothes to remain decent. The latter purpose was not a business purpose and therefore she infringed the duality of purpose rule.

Fortunately, the Taxman is rarely as strict as this in his approach and often allows expenses where they have a clear business purpose - providing there is no other purpose which is obvious. But watch out - if you press too hard you must remember that at the end of the day the Taxman could simply say the magic words "duality of purpose" and your claim will be blocked.

Don't be led into making general statements which indicate dual purpose for any expenditure. Provided the primary purpose of the expenditure was wholly and exclusively business, it does not matter that you derive some personal benefit from it - that will not preclude a tax deduction.

What matters is that the expenditure was not incurred for the purpose of getting the private benefit as well.

EXAMPLE

If you have to go to France during the summer to see a client or otherwise for a bona fide business purpose, you may as well enjoy yourself in your spare time. This does not matter providing this was not one of the reasons for going. It was just a fortuitous and pleasant side effect. During an investigation don't be drawn into admitting that you thought it would be a good place to have a good time as well, because this will prejudice your tax deduction.

Rule of thumb. If the personal benefit is just a fortuitous and pleasant side effect of an otherwise bona fide business expense, your "dual purpose" expenses will be allowed for tax. Don't be misled into saying otherwise.

3.4.   EXPENSE CLAIMS

Expenses that straddle the border between business and personal pose the highest enquiry risk. Examples include: travel, meals, entertainment, business mileage, home offices, insurance, and phone costs. These are examined by the Taxman in every full enquiry, since he suspects you are deducting personal costs, however unfair that appears to you and us.

One simple key to protecting these deductions is to first highlight any special record-keeping requirements for these expenses. This can provide an opportunity for making your return enquiry-proof - even for items well into the grey area between business and personal.

When the Taxman's manuals set specific paperwork requirements for a deduction and you meet them, a tax inspector normally has little real incentive to enquire further - and a real incentive not to, since they are under pressure to close cases and collect more tax as soon as possible.

EXAMPLE

If your records for meals show, if relevant, whom you entertained, when, where, the business purpose and the amount, then an inspector is very unlikely to insist on verification that you really discussed business at the meal. To do so wouldn't be cost-effective and would add to the backlog of cases - so with this level of record keeping you can expect the deduction to be allowed. Virtually enquiry-proof.

If the Taxman starts off examining records that are full and complete, then moves on to other items that are less than perfect examples (but still professionally presented), he is likely to review the latter in a manner that still leads to a satisfactory enquiry result because:

Reason 1

The overall quality of the records indicates that you aren't trying to "get away with something", so suspicions are not aroused.

Reason 2

High quality records increase your chance of success at an appeal, should you go there. The Taxman knows this and so has a practical reason to give enough to avoid an appeal.

Reason 3

When you present records in good order, you are being considerate, helping the Taxman to do his job - and it's human nature for consideration to be returned, as well as allowing penalties to be reduced.

However, there are two easy ways to lose the enquiry-proofing that good records can give:

1. No matter how complete your records are, the Taxman is going to have a hard time believing deductions which push the rules too far. For example, claiming three meals a day, business mileage seven days a week and work expenses for 52 weeks a year. These only invite questions about your honesty that good records are meant to prevent. So claim less than the full whack, e.g. a claim for 48 weeks allows for holidays.

2. Another way to make excellent records worthless, is to show the Taxman that they might be false. For example, online route planners and car maintenance records often snag those who exaggerate business mileage records in their diaries. So make sure you don't get caught out by this.

It's worth spending the time now annotating your expense claims as to their business purpose. Then you can direct the Taxman to your best documented deductions first and hopefully reduce the risk of a detailed enquiry.

3.5.   VALUING AN EXPENSE/BENEFIT-IN-KIND

If you want an expense to be taxed as a benefit-in-kind instead, then the contract with the supplier of the goods/services needs to be negotiated by, addressed to and be clearly a liability of the company (not yours). Otherwise the company is settling one of your liabilities and this can be reclassed by the Taxman as earnings with extra tax and NI to pay.

Where there is a benefit-in-kind, the taxable value is the "cost" the company incurs to provide the benefit rather than the market value of the goods/services.

TIP

Don't engineer a pre-set figure or just estimate based on a few facts. This will leave you open to a benefit figure being imposed by the Taxman, and in the absence of other facts he may just use a price that pushes up the value of the benefit.

However, based on a tax case, you can use marginal cost to your company rather than a wholesale price or full cost. This means that you use just the additional cost of providing you with the benefit. For example, this would be the cost of purchasing the goods, plus any costs that vary in accordance with the quantity of goods purchased, for example, delivery charges, etc. However, you don't need to take account of fixed costs, such as rent etc.

Remember. There are, of course, no benefits to be entered for those employees earning less than £8,500 p.a.

3.6.   THE THIRD UMPIRE

If the Taxman doesn't accept your arguments about expenses and you think you have a good case, you can threaten to take this before the First-Tier Tax Tribunal. This will test how strong a case the Taxman thinks he has.

But first write to the Taxman and ask him why he thinks he can take this contrary view. If nothing comes of this after 28 days, then write a letter to the District Inspector requesting that he review your case. It may be that a more experienced pair of eyes sees that a common sense approach is needed.

Again if nothing happens, then push the Taxman to focus on the facts by asking for a hearing before a tax tribunal. In the same letter, send him a draft statement of agreed facts and documentation for agreement prior to that hearing. (The costs of an appeal to a tax tribunal are likely to be prohibitive so only use this tactic to get him to move from his incorrect position.)

As a compromise before actually going to the tribunal, you could ask for the enquiry to be closed at a figure somewhere between his and yours. If he refuses, ask for a "closure review" by another officer. If this doesn't get you the figure you want, you then have to decide whether you actually go to tribunal.

3.7.   WHAT IF YOU JUST TRUST TO LUCK?

3.7.1.   Feeling lucky?

For the high-risk rollers there is an alternative approach, and that's the simple "hide it and hope" option. What this entails is putting purely personal expenses through the business in the hope that they stay hidden, and tackling the Taxman as and when he comes looking.

3.7.2.   What are the penalties if discovered?

This is potentially an expensive strategy. Not only could it leave you with a nasty tax bill, it could also give rise to what the Taxman calls "culpable penalties", which is basically a fine for not getting things right in the first place.

A new penalty regime for errors on any returns made to the Taxman (including P11Ds) commenced on April 1 2009. Mistakes on returns are now penalised depending on the behaviour which led to the inaccuracy.

1. Innocent mistake

Where you have taken reasonable care to ensure that a return doesn't understate the tax due, there will be no penalty. People do make mistakes, but provided you have taken reasonable care, an innocent mistake will not be punished.

2. Lack of reasonable care

Where the error arises through carelessness, and you did not take sufficient care over preparing a particular return, you will be liable to a penalty of 30% of the tax understated.

Note. Where you confess and notify HMRC of the error, it's possible to significantly reduce the rate of penalty. Depending on the circumstances it can be reduced to nil in the case of an unprompted disclosure, and 15% if the disclosure was prompted by HMRC.

3. Dishonesty

If you were to deliberately claim private expenses as business ones, the penalties range from 70% for deliberate understatements to 100% for deliberate understatements that have been concealed. Again, larger reductions are available for unprompted full disclosure rather than after a request for information by HMRC.

TIP

You are expected to keep sufficient records on which to base a return. Beyond that, seek advice if you are unsure about something, and if you remain unsure, disclose that uncertainty on the return.

3.7.3.   Leave it all to your accountant?

When you have an accountant there is potentially more scope for error in terms of a breakdown in communication. The good news is that there is no penalty for careless error when the return is dealt with by an accountant if HMRC is satisfied that you took reasonable care but the accountant just made a silly mistake.

3.7.4. How much?

The Taxman claims that there is no difference between his old penalty regime and the new one, in that penalties can range from 0% of the tax involved, for wholly innocent errors, up to 100% for deliberate and concealed actions to reduce the tax payable.

EXAMPLE

During a compliance visit the Taxman calculated that the company had over-claimed £10,000 of expenses against Corporation Tax. After review, HMRC calculated that the tax due was £2,400. It then issued a penalty notice to the company charging them £1,680 (70% of the tax due). Hence a total bill of £4,080.

The change

When it comes to tax errors, HMRC is now taking a tough line on small amounts. Previously, a penalty in excess of 50% was rare and usually involved large sums of tax and deliberate actions on the part of the taxpayer.

Of course, it is possible to appeal against any penalty issued. However, it is becoming clearer that the smaller sums involved might not make it cost effective for a taxpayer to do so, once professional fees for fighting your corner are taken into account.

From April 2009, HMRC has also been offering the option of an internal review of tax decisions with the aim of *"resolving issues as quickly as possible"*. One Taxman checking another's work? Not exactly independent, is it?

3.7.5. Will you be interviewed by the Taxman?

Generally speaking, a meeting with the Taxman is not required. However, where you've gone down the route of "hide it and hope" with personal expenses, the chances of being called for one increases once you've been discovered. The important rules to remember with interviews are:

- consider having the meeting at your premises: being on familiar territory can give you a big advantage
- be co-operative: any penalties could be reduced as a result
- rehearse your responses. That way he's less likely to trick you into saying the wrong thing
- give full explanations but be concise. If you tell him too much it could open up further questions.

Remember, the Taxman's a civil servant, not a crown barrister or MI5 agent. He may be more experienced in these matters but he can only make a judgement on the information he has in front of him. Only you know the real facts; don't let him try to convince you otherwise.

3.7.6. Can the Taxman look at other years?

If the Taxman finds problems in one year, he's going to assume the same thing applied in the past. But don't just let him widen his enquiry into earlier years. Ask him why he wants this information and under what authority he's asking for it; remember, the Taxman has strict rules to follow, he can't just go marching in to your premises and make unreasonable demands.

3.7.7. When do you negotiate?

Negotiation needs to be done before a Taxman's enquiry is closed and payment is being sought. What you need is a counter-argument, e.g. expenses or capital allowances that you didn't claim before, which may come to light if you go through your records in as much detail as he does.

> **TIP**
>
> With the Taxman, you have to negotiate when the enquiry is still open, not when it's time to pay.

3.7.8. How will you know if the enquiry is finished?

When he's made his enquiries and you've answered his questions, get him to close the case as quickly as possible. There's no point in you running up extra interest costs at his convenience. Once the final bill comes, check his calculations to make sure they tally to the figures you supplied.

If there are penalties, remember that there's a discretionary element to this and it's possible to negotiate them down. Point out that you've been co-operative and that any errors were genuine mistakes.

Once the amount of tax due has been transferred to the so-called Receivables Managers, the stated policy is now "pay up or else". So expect requests for time to pay/paying by instalments to be met with comments like "well can't you borrow the money from someone else?". Don't be bullied, push for instalments and the official rate of interest on overdue amounts.

KEY POINTS

- the Taxman will want to disallow expenses if they are not "wholly and exclusively" for the benefit of the trade
- provided the primary purpose of the expense was wholly and exclusively business, it doesn't matter that you derive some personal benefit from it
- any note of a meeting made at the time or shortly afterwards can be produced as evidence in a dispute
- don't give in to all his demands without question. Check his results to see that they agree with the facts
- if the Taxman doesn't accept your arguments about expenses and you think you have a good case, you can threaten to take it to the tax tribunal. This will test how strong a case the Taxman thinks he has.

Regardless of the sums involved, when looking at what penalty to impose for a mistake on an expense claim the Taxman will be looking to see if:

- your company has taken due care and attention
- the mistake is deliberate or not; and
- records have been kept correctly.

CHAPTER 4

Your expenses claim

4.1. INTRODUCTION

There are few things more tedious than filling out expenses claim forms, particularly if this includes rustling through drawers and wallets to fish out old receipts and keeping track of how many miles you've travelled. In an ideal world you would be able to get all suppliers to bill your company directly, and it pay them directly. That way you would never have to fill out a form to be reimbursed for expenses you have incurred on the company's behalf. However, try asking your taxi driver to invoice your company. It just doesn't work like that for certain expenses. And so you will still end up paying for some things with your own cash.

Then there's the Taxman's interest in all of this. First off, for each tax year your company has an obligation to provide certain information regarding expenses to both the Taxman and its own employees. It does so via Forms P11D, for all directors plus employees earning more than £8,500 a year. Collecting and analysing the information for P11Ds can be an onerous task, and the penalties for getting it wrong are potentially very high. Analysing a year's worth of your employees' expenses claim forms is very time-consuming, but necessary, unless you have a dispensation in place (see Chapter 6).

Secondly, if there is ever a records inspection by the Taxman, he will want to see your expenses claim forms with receipts attached; he will also check that the reimbursements on the company bank statements match the amounts claimed on the expenses forms. In addition, he will expect to find that the procedures for submitting and authorising expenses claims have been well documented and communicated to employees.

Your company's expenses claim forms, correctly completed, are, therefore, key documents for each tax year.

4.2. STANDARD CLAIM FORMS

It makes practical sense to have your company's form designed in such a way that the claimant supplies all the information needed to process the expenses claim quickly and accurately. The process of making a claim includes signing a form, attaching receipts for individual claims and passing it to a director or a line manager for approval. Once you have the form in a format which you are happy with, stick with it! That way, you and your staff will become accustomed to the process.

Download Zone

For an **Expenses Claim Form**, visit **http://books.indicator.co.uk**. You'll find the access code on page 2 of this book.

4.2.1. Date column

For most expenses, e.g. subsistence, entertaining, enter the date they were incurred. However, if you are claiming for a return journey which is covered by one receipt/ticket, enter the date of the outward journey in the date field and note the return journey in the description field.

4.2.2. Details to support the claim

Descriptions need only be brief. For example, *"Flight to London for XYZ Conference"*, or "Sandwich lunch". If you feel you need to give more detail, attach a note to the expenses claim form.

When it comes to claims for business mileage in your own car, a simple *"Birmingham to Newcastle (200 miles)"* would suffice. The detail can be provided on an attached mileage record form.

Download Zone

For a **Mileage Record**, visit **http://books.indicator.co.uk**. You'll find the access code on page 2 of this book.

We recommend that mileage is claimed at the Taxman's approved rate. These rates had been the same for several years up to and including 2010/11; however, for 2011/12 they have been increased to:

- 45p per mile - first 10,000 miles per tax year

- 25p per mile - additional miles.

These rates are supposed to cover all the conceivable running costs of having a car. That means that you or your company have to keep a log of all of your business journeys in your own car so that you don't pay the wrong rate when the 10,000 milestone is breached.

The VAT on fuel can be reclaimed, but beware that the total fuel costs may be less than the total claim for mileage. You can only claim back actual VAT incurred, and not notional VAT based on the Taxman's rate.

VAT warning. If you pay a mileage allowance to your employees for business journeys made in either their own vehicle or a company car, you can reclaim VAT on only the fuel element of those mileage payments. (For more details on this see Chapter 7.)

4.2.3. Total including VAT

As a director/employee you are claiming back all of the gross amounts including VAT on your expenses claim form. Leave the VAT reclaim to the experts.

4.2.4. VAT recoverable column

It's the Company's accountant/bookkeeper who needs to know which items on the expenses claim form include VAT and which don't. That's why you should attach receipts to the claim form for everything that's bought on behalf of the business.

TIP

It's best if original receipts accompany all claims. Credit card slips or statements will not generally be accepted by the Taxman as evidence of business expenditure.

A valid VAT receipt must include:

- the name and address of the retailer
- the retailer's VAT registration number
- the date of purchase
- details of what goods or services have been purchased; and
- the VAT-inclusive value of those goods or services in sterling.

Note. A VAT registration number consists of nine digits and is set out in the following format: 123 4567 89.

TIP

In order to recover the VAT you are charged you should obtain a VAT invoice, although for supplies of less than £250 (excluding VAT) you only need a "less detailed" tax invoice.

4.2.5. Accounts use

Detail codes can be used to assign expenditure to the correct category for accounting purposes, so you should select the one which matches the expenditure you have made. If you don't know what that is, speak to your accountant. Expenses codes do not tend to change, so once you know the relevant cost centre(s), you can put them at the foot of the relevant column of your company's expenses claim form.

4.2.6. Declaration box

The Taxman likes to see that you have an independent system in place to check claims and deductions. The simplest evidence of this is to include a "declaration box" at the foot of the form where the employee certifies that the expenses claimed have been necessarily incurred on the company's business. For example:

Declaration

I certify that the above expenditure has necessarily been incurred on the Company's business as shown above.

Signed..

Date ....

Authorised .... Director/Manager

Note. The expenses claim is countersigned by a (fellow) director or manager of the claimant. When they sign off, authorising directors/managers are saying to the Taxman "look no further" we are happy with the business nature of the claim, otherwise we would have rejected it for correction or further information. In fact, it doesn't do any harm to have significant claims or items show an additional authorisation by the finance or managing director.

You can submit a claim as soon as the expenses have been incurred. However, it costs a certain amount of admin time to process any claim.

4.3. GUIDANCE FOR EMPLOYEES

The Taxman would expect to find that the procedures for submitting and authorising expenses claims have been well documented and communicated to employees. You, on the other hand, might not feel that training is required to teach a member of staff how to fill in an expenses claim form. However, new employees will not be familiar with the company's expenses policy or what cost centre codes to use or even what to do about the VAT element. You can safely bet that the Taxman assumes new employees will make mistakes so he will target these during a review - after he's singled out the directors, of course.

TIP

Anticipate this by including a session on how expenses are claimed in new employee inductions. This will hopefully prevent either you or your accountant from having to redo their first few expenses claims or dealing with the Taxman's questions.

Your company expenses policy will tell your employees (and the Taxman) all they need to know about your procedures for dealing with certain types of expense.

Download Zone

For an **Expenses Policy**, visit **http://books.indicator.co.uk**. You'll find the access code on page 2 of this book.

4.4. EXPENSES IN FOREIGN CURRENCIES

Do you need a separate claim form for expenses in a foreign currency? Not really; instead you simply use the same claim form just converting the foreign currency amount to its sterling equivalent. However, a visiting Taxman (if he looked) would expect to find evidence of the exchange rate you have used, for example a currency exchange slip or copy of the web page from which you have obtained the exchange rate, as well as receipts for the purchases themselves.

TIP

With foreign expenses payments enter the amount you are claiming in sterling and note the exchange rate used in the description field. For example, *"Train from Lyon to Paris; £1.00 = €1.20"*.

What if you used your personal credit card to make expenses payments in foreign currencies? Best practice suggests that you have two options:

Option 1

Wait until your credit card statement arrives and claim the amount in sterling that appears. Attach a copy of your credit card statement (with personal purchases blacked out) as well as receipts for the purchases with your expenses claim form.

Option 2

If you can't wait for your credit card statement, attach the receipts for your purchases to your claim form and convert them to sterling at a particular rate. However, this may mean that you will receive a different exchange rate to the one on your credit card either in your favour or not.

4.5.   START-UP EXPENSES

What normally happens to a new business is that you have expenses which you want to reclaim before you have any funds to pay them. There are two ways to handle this dilemma.

1.   Wait until the business can afford to make the reimbursement.

2.   Introduce working capital (of your own) into the business, and then reimburse yourself.

The second one sounds odd, but at least you build up the bank transactions that you're looking for. Over the course of the financial year these movements of capital accumulate and are shown in the annual accounts as a loan from the director to the company. Take care, because this can sometimes work the other way. If you take too much capital out of the company, the loan is the other way around and there can be adverse tax consequences.

KEY POINTS

Standardisation

- use a standardised expenses claim form
- VAT included
- as a director/employee you are claiming back all the gross amounts including VAT on your expenses claim form. Leave the VAT reclaim to the experts
- in order to recover the VAT you should obtain a VAT invoice, although for supplies of less than £250 excluding VAT you only need a "less detailed" tax invoice.

Signed declaration

- have all expenses claims authorised by a fellow director/senior manager who is familiar with the claimant's work schedule. Their signature indicates they are happy with the claim. Certain claims or items may require additional authorisation by the finance director or managing director.

Guidance

- the Taxman would expect to find that the procedures for submitting and authorising expenses claims have been well documented and communicated to employees
- your company expenses policy will tell your employees (and the Taxman) all they need to know about your procedures for dealing with certain types of expenses
- the Taxman assumes that new employees make mistakes and he will target these during a review. Anticipate this and include how expenses are claimed in the employee's induction.

Expenses in foreign currencies

- with expenses payments in foreign currencies use the same claim form, converting the foreign currency amount to its sterling equivalent. However, as well as receipts for the purchases themselves attach evidence of the exchange rate you have used.

CHAPTER 5

Your company's expenses policy

5.1. INTRODUCTION

The Taxman regards expense claims as the front line when it comes to the battle to prevent private expenditure being smuggled into the company's books under the guise of "business expenses". Having a suitable expenses policy in your company (and enforcing it) goes a long way in convincing a suspicious Taxman to look somewhere else for unpaid tax. Given this fact, it's surprising that a survey of business indicated that only just over half of small companies and business start-ups have a formal expenses policy in place, leaving themselves open to errors, a potential tax bill and unnecessary (or even fraudulent) spending. Is your business one of them?

Download Zone

For an **Expenses Policy**, visit **http://books.indicator.co.uk**. You'll find the access code on page 2 of this book.

5.2. COMPANY MONEY

Why would the Taxman think that expense claims are open to abuse? Human nature is the answer, as the results of a recent survey indicate. It found that 60% of employees said they were able to claim expenses without receipts at least some of the time, while nearly a fifth (18%) thought it was acceptable to exaggerate claims. But this means there is some good news, with 82% of staff saying they thought it unacceptable to exaggerate claims. However, over half thought people became more lax in their attitude towards employee expenses the longer they have been with a company.

The Taxman is well aware of this varying attitude towards spending company money and so would expect a company to take tighter control over its expense management policies.

TIP

Have a well publicised expenses policy to encourage compliance among employees. By monitoring and analysing employee spending, you can piece together a complete picture of your company's expenditure and begin to negotiate better deals with suppliers, as well as stamp out any unauthorised spending.

5.3. IS THE POLICY ENFORCED?

Sometimes company expenses policies don't reflect reality and need to be updated.

But far more frequently they aren't followed because employees are unaware of them and managers don't bother to enforce them. One report examined 3,530,000 individual expenses claims from over 60,000 companies and found that £1.3 billion is paid out to employees every year for money supposedly spent on behalf of the company.

Successful claims included money spent on lap-dancers, condoms and cat food. You can easily imagine some managers allowing an erroneous claim for £470 on a £4.70 travel cost. The combined cost to UK businesses from "out-of-policy" claims that were approved and other expenses fraud is £1.284 billion: about £500 per expense-claiming employee.

EXAMPLE

If 18% of your staff thought it was acceptable to exaggerate expenses claims, then of the, say, £50,000 you paid in total as expenses last year, £9,000 could have been due to fraudulent claims. If the Taxman gets hold of this he will be asking for £1,800 in Corporation Tax plus penalties and interest. And then he'll ramp up his calculation by extrapolating this to earlier years.

You won't be able to prevent all private expenses from being claimed as business ones. No company is perfect in this respect. However, what you can do is reduce the risk by having a clear, well-publicised expenses policy that is enforced by your managers.

TIP

Remind managers and staff from time to time that they have no authority to vary the company's expenses policy. Any out-of-policy claims will ultimately be rejected. Point out that failure to comply with this policy may be treated as a disciplinary matter.

5.4. WHAT SHOULD YOU INCLUDE IN THE POLICY?

5.4.1. General principles

You should start by explaining some general principles that underlie the policy. Something simple will do, along the lines of *"The principle of the Expenses Policy is to reimburse directors and employees for all expenditure reasonably incurred in the performance of their Company duties".*

Then go on to remind claimants that the basis of expense claims will be actual expenditure up to limits specified in the policy. You'll set these based on a combination of how much you consider reasonable and the tax-free amount the Taxman will let the company get away with.

5.4.2.   Timeliness of submission

Expenses can be submitted as soon as they have been incurred. However, it costs a certain amount to process any claim, so claimants should be discouraged from submitting a large number of small claims. You could specify in the policy that expenses claims can only be made monthly. Indeed, to avoid any late adjustments to the expenses shown in your monthly management accounts, tell claimants to submit their claims for a particular month by, say, the second week of the following month.

Tip

Consider reimbursing employees' expenses once a month together with their salary payment through the payroll.

5.4.3.   Receipts

It's best if you specify that original receipts should accompany all claims. Point out that credit card slips or statements are not generally accepted by the Taxman as evidence of business expenditure.

As a VAT-registered business you can maximise the amount of input VAT that your company can claim back on expenses if you ask the claimant to attach valid VAT receipts. Remember to specify what you consider to be a VAT receipt. For example, it must include the name and address of the retailer, the retailer's VAT registration number, the date of the purchase, details of what goods or services have been purchased and the VAT-inclusive value of those goods or services in sterling. A VAT registration number consists of nine digits and is set out in the following format: 123 4567 89.

Tip

For expenditure on an item or service of less than £250 (excluding VAT), a less detailed tax invoice will suffice.

5.4.4. Authorisation of expenses

All expense claims must be authorised by a more senior manager who is familiar with the claimant's work schedule. Tell the authorising managers that they must make sure they are happy with the claim, or reject it for correction or further information. Certain claims or items may require additional authorisation by the finance director.

5.5. EXPENSE CATEGORIES

If you have categories of expense that are regularly claimed, then consider writing a paragraph on each in the main body of your policy.

These may include:

- motoring
- entertaining
- working from home
- subsistence
- overseas expenses
- professional fees and subscriptions
- telephone calls
- accommodation
- fares and travel.

CHAPTER 6

Current dispensation process

6.1. INTRODUCTION

Tax legislation specifies that expenses payments reimbursed to an employee, for example, travel expenses, course fees, the cost of entertaining clients, represent taxable earnings and need to be reported to the Taxman. The employee can then submit a claim under s.336 of the **Income Tax (Earnings and Pensions) Act 2003** that an expense should not be taxable because it was incurred *"wholly, exclusively and necessarily in the performance of their duties of employment"*.

Any expenses payments made to a higher-paid employee or director during a tax year are reported on a Form P11D. A higher-paid employee is one earning more than £8,500 a year (including benefits and expenses). For lower-paid employees, a simpler version of the form, known as a P9D, is used. Copies of the form must be provided to the Taxman and to the employee after the tax year has closed.

This requirement for reporting (by the employer) and then claiming (by the employee) for business expenses payments as non-taxable can be particularly burdensome. This is often made worse by the difficulty in getting the expenses payments correctly reflected in an employee's PAYE tax code. You can ease this burden by applying for a reporting dispensation. This is an agreement with the Taxman that removes the requirement to report certain expenses on Forms P11D. Expenses covered by a dispensation are not liable to tax or Class 1 or 1A NI contributions.

So what will the Taxman issue a dispensation for and how easy is it to get one?

6.2. WHICH EXPENSES ARE ELIGIBLE?

A dispensation can apply to all expenses for which the employee would normally be able to claim as being "wholly, exclusively and necessarily" incurred. These would typically include: travel and subsistence; business entertaining; and professional fees and subscriptions. Currently, a dispensation doesn't cover: company cars and vans; private medical insurance and cheap loans. These still need to be reported on a P11D.

It's also worth mentioning that payments to employees who use their own cars for business travel (see Chapter 7) don't require a dispensation if your company doesn't pay more than the published statutory rates.

When applying for a dispensation, the Taxman will seek confirmation that you have an independent system in place to check claims and deductions. This can often cause problems for smaller businesses, although it should still be possible to obtain a dispensation, provided that valid receipts are retained in support of all expenses.

In general, dispensations take effect from the date on which the Taxman issues them.

However, he can agree that your dispensation can take effect from the beginning of the tax year in which you apply for it. What you can't get is a dispensation issued retrospectively for an earlier year.

6.3.   HOW DO YOU APPLY?

To apply for a dispensation you simply need to supply details of expenses and benefit payments to the Taxman. There are two ways to do this: either using an online form or the paper equivalent. In either case, the Taxman aims to respond within 15 working days.

6.3.1.   Applying by post

To apply by post you need to print off and then complete Form P11DX "Dispensation for expenses payments and benefits in kind", from HMRC's website: http://hmrc. gov.uk/forms/p11dx.pdf.

Send it to:

HMRC
Local Compliance
Specialist Employer Compliance
Bowback House
299 Silbury Boulevard
Witan Gate West
Milton Keynes
Buckinghamshire
MK9 1NG

Copy of expenses policy. In the guidance to the manual version of the P11DX the Taxman politely asks that if you have "any notes for guidance on employees' expenses" to enclose a copy with the form. And if that isn't enough additional information, he will "tell you if any further information is required".

6.3.2.   Applying online

The Taxman is publicly seeking to encourage the use of dispensations and to this aim he recently added a facility to the HMRC website enabling dispensations to be applied for online. See http://www.hmrc.gov.uk/online/.

This largely mirrors the manual application process so you can get a good idea of what is expected by reading through the online questions. You mostly tick the relevant check box(es) and ignore any that don't apply. The help icons next to the answers you are expected to give are embedded links to the Taxman's "A-Z of Expenses and benefits", see http://www.hmrc.gov.uk/paye/exb/a-z/a/index.htm.

Tɪᴘ

You can't save your progress and return to it at a later time, so you'll need to have all your answers ready beforehand. Do this by printing off what you can see on the screen and annotating this hard copy with your own queries and final answers. Only answer the questions that are relevant to you and leave blank any that don't apply.

Electronic receipt

If you provide an e-mail address, the Taxman will acknowledge that he has received your application. This acknowledgement service is not available for manually submitted applications.

6.4.   WHAT QUESTIONS DOES THE TAXMAN CURRENTLY ASK?

The online form specifically asks about the following expenses:

- travel, including subsistence costs associated with business travel
- fuel for company cars
- hire car costs
- expenses paid/reimbursed for use of telephone(s)
- expenses paid for a dedicated landline at home
- entertainment expenses
- company credit/charge cards
- fees and subscriptions to professional bodies
- other expenses.

There is also room on the form to add other business-related expenses not already listed which you want covered by the dispensation.

6.4.1.   Declaration

There are two key questions at the end of the form. First, you'll be asked to declare whether or not you always obtain invoices/receipts for all claims? The Taxman is looking for a "Yes" answer here.

Then comes the second question which is about independent checking of expense claims. The Taxman again is expecting a "Yes" answer. He is primarily looking for a system that will ensure the rules of the dispensation are followed, i.e. with more than one person always examining claims to verify that they don't include items which are not allowable under tax/NI legislation.

He may therefore try to reject a dispensation claim for a director who checks their own expenses.

TIP

If yours is a one-man company, your accountant could provide a checking service; once a year may be sufficient where only a small volume of expenses are incurred.

When you sign the application you do so believing that the information you have given is "correct and complete" to the best of your knowledge and belief.

6.4.2. Which employees are to be covered?

You can include as many employees and/or directors as you want in your dispensation application. Online you are asked to select from one of the following categories:

- all employees and all directors
- all employees but not directors
- all directors
- a specific group of employees, e.g. sales team; or
- employees seconded to work in the United Kingdom.

If you go for "A specific group of employees", there's a box for you to put a name to that group e.g. the sales team.

TIP

You can apply for more than one dispensation for your company, e.g. travel and subsistence for directors, hire cars for the sales team.

TIP

Remember that the answer you give on the form must relate to all of the people you've included in the "Employee details" section.

6.4.3. Requests for further information

If the completed Form P11DX is not enough, then the Taxman will write to your company asking for further information. Let's say you have applied for a dispensation for the usual items, e.g. business travel, subsistence, accommodation, telephone calls etc., and have provided details of your company's expenses procedures, e.g. what can be claimed, authorisation and sign off procedures etc.

In response, you might well receive a questionnaire (a three-page letter) from the Taxman asking 20 questions under the headings of *"General"*, *"Travel"*, *"Subsistence"* and *"Entertaining"* to enable him "to further consider the request". The information requested on the questionnaire/letter might seem no different to a PAYE compliance inspection which would also ask for expenses claim sheets and trading information for the latest tax year.

TIP

If you receive the questionnaire, ring the Taxman and explain that you have already provided the information with your original application.

TIP

On the basis of what you tell him the Taxman needs to be satisfied that no additional tax would be payable by the employee concerned. So vet the answers you plan on giving with this in mind.

6.5. WHAT IF YOU ARE SUCCESSFUL?

If you are successful in your application for a dispensation then you will get a letter from the Taxman confirming this and enclosing the Dispensation Notice itself.

Download Zone

For a **Sample Dispensation Notice**, visit **http://books.indicator.co.uk**. You'll find the access code on page 2 of this book.

Warning. The Taxman can withdraw dispensations if it appears to him that they are not being correctly administered, e.g. it's being applied to expenditure not part of the original agreement. In early 2008 HMRC announced that where it considers the terms of a dispensation are not being adhered to, it will revoke it retrospectively. This would mean having to complete Forms P11D for all the previous years affected. Worse still, it could result in additional PAYE and NI liabilities, penalties and interest charges.

Current dispensation process

6

Check the operation of your dispensation each year. To do this you will only need to review a one-in-ten sample of your records to prove that the terms you agreed have been followed correctly. Keep a copy of the checks to show the Taxman.

6.6. REVIEW OF "OLD" DISPENSATIONS BY THE TAXMAN

If your company has been in business for a number of years, you might have a Dispensation Notice which is more than six years old. If so, it's more than likely you will receive a letter from the Taxman about reviewing it. It will say that he needs to carry out "routine checks" to make sure the dispensation is still needed and that you are still meeting the terms. To help him with his check you are asked to complete a new P11DX either online or by post.

In the examples of recent requests that we have seen the Taxman then asks you to supply a copy of an employee's completed expenses claim form for the last month, or for the most recent period that you have. You need to send it to the address at the top of his letter.

He will also set a date by which you have to supply him with what has been requested; it's usually six weeks from the date of his letter.

Example

C Ltd's Dispensation Notice was issued to it by the Taxman on June 13 2001. The expenses it referred to were: travel and subsistence; mileage payments; entertainment and telephones. It only took up half a page of text. In mid-July 2010 they received a Review of Dispensation letter dated July 2 2010 with a date for complying with it of August 13 2010. They chose to submit a P11DX by post rather than online, as this also allowed them to submit the requested copy of a completed expenses claim for June 2010 at the same time.

Their existing Notice did not cover them for paying professional fees and subscriptions, so they answered the relevant section of the P11DX to have this included, which it duly was in the new Dispensation Notice issued to them on September 7 2010.

Tip

Pick a recent expenses claim to copy and submit that is typical but does not contain any items that the Taxman would consider contentious.

TIP

This is also your opportunity to revise your dispensation and add items. Simply tell the Taxman what you need by ticking the appropriate box on the P11DX or by entering it in the section headed "Other expenses".

KEY POINTS

The application

- you can apply for a dispensation at any time via the Taxman's online form or by post. In either case, the Taxman aims to respond within 15 working days. If you apply by post, this allows you to attach a copy of both your expenses policy and claim form, the submission of which should stop a request for further information.

Effective date

- in general, dispensations take effect from the date on which the Taxman issues them. However, he can agree that your dispensation can take effect from the beginning of the tax year in which you apply for it. You can't obtain a dispensation for an earlier year.

Avoid being out-of-date

- check the operation of your dispensation each year. To do this you will only need to review a one-in-ten sample of your records to prove that the terms you agreed have been followed correctly. Keep a copy of the checks to show the Taxman.

CHAPTER 7

Mileage allowance

7.1. THE EXPENSE

You can claim for any costs relating to business journeys and associated travel. This includes travel to a temporary workplace. However, any reimbursement for a journey that is ordinary commuting or non-business travel should have tax and NI deducted from it.

7.2. BUSINESS JOURNEYS

As far as the Taxman is concerned, business journeys only include those:

- forming part of an employee's employment duties, such as between appointments or to external meetings
- related to an employee's attendance at a temporary workplace.

If your destination is further from your home than your normal place of work, the claimable mileage is the lower of the distance: **(1)** from your home to your temporary destination; or **(2)** from your normal place of work to the temporary destination. This is sometimes referred to as the triangulation rule.

7.3. COSTS INCURRED

Own car

When driving on company business we recommend that mileage is claimed at the HMRC approved rate. However, for 2011/12 these are now:

- 45p (previously 40p per mile) - first 10,000 miles per year
- 25p per mile - additional miles.

This rate is to cover all the conceivable running costs of a car. No other motoring costs can be claimed from your company.

If the Taxman starts asking questions about the accuracy of your business mileage claim, there is an easy way to satisfy his curiosity.

You simply provide a detailed mileage log of all business journeys. If you can't don't worry, because it's possible to get the Taxman to accept, albeit reluctantly, a sample log for a defined period, or indirect records, e.g. a diary showing the date and destination of journeys, from which mileage can be worked out. He has been known to use a web-based route finder to check distances used in expenses claims. So if you're not sure of the mileage, use one yourself.

You might have the mileage records in a diary or a notebook. It's best to transfer this to a mileage log showing the date of the mileage and the purpose of the trip - just in case there's anything else in the notebook that you wouldn't want the Taxman to see.

As the tax-free rates change depending on the number of miles completed in a tax year, you also need to have procedures in place to keep track of the number of miles claimed by each employee. One way of doing this is by getting employees to fill out a monthly mileage record in addition to their expenses claim form.

Download Zone

For a **Mileage Record**, visit **http://books.indicator.co.uk**. You'll find the access code on page 2 of this book.

Company car

If you have a company car for business use, the Taxman will only let you reclaim the fuel element of the mileage costs. This is because the company is able to claim a tax deduction for the other running costs elsewhere in its accounts. The current rates are from March 1 2011. For one month from the date of change, employers may use either the previous or new current rates, as they choose. Employers may therefore make or require supplementary payments if they so wish, but are under no obligation to do so.

	UP TO 1,400cc	1,401 - 2,000cc	OVER 2,000cc
Petrol	14p	16p	23p
Diesel	13p	13p	16p
LPG	10p	12p	17p

Petrol hybrid cars are treated as petrol cars for this purpose.

TIP

The Taxman will expect company car drivers to fill out a monthly mileage record in addition to their expenses claim form.

Warning. If employees use their own vehicles for business journeys, you should also have a company car policy, which spells out the situation regarding insurance, parking and mileage rates at which you will reimburse them.

7.4. VAT RECOVERY

The VAT on fuel can be reclaimed, but you can only claim back actual VAT incurred, and not notional VAT based on the HMRC rate. For a more detailed discussion of VAT on fuel see Chapter 19.

> **TIP**
>
> Although there is no direct relationship between fuel purchases and business mileage, where possible you'll need a VAT fuel receipt in order to allow the company to recover VAT on mileage.

7.5. DISPENSATION AVAILABLE?

Dispensations are no longer needed in respect of mileage allowances paid to employees using their own vehicles for business travel. Amounts not exceeding the qualifying amount, the number of miles of business travel multiplied by the currently applicable rate, are exempt from tax. That is currently 45p (previously 40p per mile) for the first 10,000 miles per year and 25p per mile additional mile.

Obviously, amounts in excess of the approved amount are always taxable.

Business journeys

- if your destination is further from your home than your normal place of work, the claimable mileage is the lower of the distance from your home to your temporary destination, or from your normal place of work to the temporary destination.

Costs incurred

- own car - when driving your own car on company business, mileage can be claimed at the Taxman's approved rate of 45p per mile. No other motoring costs can be claimed from your company
- company car - the Taxman will only let you reclaim the fuel element of the mileage costs. This is because the company is able to claim a tax deduction for the other running costs of the car elsewhere.

VAT recovery

- the VAT on fuel can be reclaimed. However, you can only claim back the actual VAT incurred, and not notional VAT based on the Taxman's 45p per mile rate.

Dispensation

- payments to employees who use their own cars for business travel don't require a dispensation if your company doesn't pay more than the published statutory rates.
- as the tax-free rates change depending on the number of miles completed in a tax year, you also need to have mileage records for each employee.

CHAPTER 8

Other motoring expenses

8.1.   INTRODUCTION

In addition to mileage claims, there may be other items associated with either private or company cars appearing on expenses claims. So it makes sense to include something about these in your company's expenses policy, spelling out what the company will and won't reimburse.

8.2.   EXAMPLES

8.2.1.   Parking

There can be times when directors/employees have to pay for on-street or off-street parking, which they will later seek to recover from the company as a legitimate business expense.

Your company policy could probably say something simple like: *"Reasonable car parking costs while on business will be met."* Nothing more is required.

8.2.2.   Tolls and congestion charges

Your company policy could cover this by including the following paragraph: *"Necessary road and bridge toll costs will be met, including the London Congestion Charge where there is a genuine business need to incur it. No tolls or congestion charges can be claimed for travel between home and work."*

8.2.3.   Fines

You may find parking tickets are claimed for on expenses forms. These are normally the liability of the individual not the company and should not be reimbursed. However, you may wish to state in your policy: *"In exceptional cases an authorising manager may agree to reimburse a fine incurred as a result of an emergency and this should be recovered via expenses. Any such reimbursement may give rise to a tax liability."*

8.2.4. Fuel etc. for pool vehicles

Pool vehicles are those that meet the following conditions: **(1)** are used by more than one employee; **(2)** not ordinarily used by one employee to the exclusion of others; **(3)** not normally kept at or near employees' homes; **(4)** used only for business journeys - private use is only permitted if it's merely incidental to a business journey, for example taking the car home to allow an early start to a business journey the next morning.

Provided all these conditions are met, neither your company nor the director/ employee has any reporting requirements or tax and NI to pay.

If you put fuel in the tank of a pool car, then you can claim for the full amount including the VAT. There is no need to get involved with mileage rates etc.

8.3. VAT

In order to recover the VAT, you should obtain a VAT invoice. However, for the majority of other motoring expenses you are likely to encounter on expenses claims you can accept a less detailed receipt. Issued for supplies of less than £250 (excluding VAT) these less detailed VAT invoices must still have the supplier's VAT registration number on it.

TIP

If the VAT included is not shown separately on the receipt, you can legitimately calculate and claim it as 1/6th (or 20/120) of the total amount. For example, a £12 payment includes VAT of £2.

TIP

There is no need for an invoice/receipt to claim back VAT if the cost of supply is less than £25.

8.3.1. Parking

There may be VAT claimable on certain car parking charges. If there is VAT to reclaim, there will be a VAT number on the car parking receipt. You don't need an invoice/receipt to claim back the VAT on off-street parking (on-street parking is not subject to VAT) provided that the cost of the supply is £25 or less.

Note. There is no VAT to be reclaimed on parking fines, as these are outside the scope of VAT.

8.4. DISPENSATION AVAILABLE?

The Taxman's standard dispensation wording for "travel" identifies parking, road and bridge tolls as examples of minor expenditure which may be reimbursed with no further reporting required, provided there's documentation about the business journey they relate to.

Other motoring expenses

CHAPTER 9

UK fares and travel

9.1. INTRODUCTION

The definition of a business journey is where as part of your job you have to travel from one workplace to another (including travelling between your main permanent workplace and a temporary one), or where you have to travel to and from a workplace because your job requires you to. However, business journeys don't include ordinary commuting or private journeys.

Travel expenses that qualify for tax relief for your company include: rail fares, air fares, public transport fares, taxi fares, hotel accommodation (see Chapter 12); meals (see Chapter 10) and business phone calls, fax or photocopying costs (see Chapter 17).

You might have to use your own car, van, motorbike or bicycle to make business journeys. In that case your company can make mileage allowance payments to cover your costs and you don't have to pay tax on this (see Chapter 7).

9.2. TAXI FARES

The cost of taxi fares to and from business meetings is allowable against your company's profits. However, the Taxman sometimes asks whether any transport has been provided for a director's ordinary commuting, e.g. taxi fare home.

Paying for your ordinary commuting home to work or vice versa, normally produces a tax charge. It's private travel, and so taxable on you - with Class 1A employers' NI for the company.

There is no realistic offsetting claim that can be made under the "by reason of my employment" banner. But there is a tax concession you can rely on to potentially get around this occasional problem.

The terms of the concession are that: **(1)** you're required to work at least until 9pm; **(2)** this is not a regular requirement; **(3)** no more than 60 such journeys in a tax year; **(4)** public transport has ceased or it's not reasonable to use it; and **(5)** it must be a taxi, hired car or similar private transport.

As long as the terms of the concession are met, you don't need to include the cost of the transport for PAYE purposes or show it on a P11D. You don't need to get a specific dispensation from the Taxman either. Employees just leave these payments off their tax return.

TIP

If you are working late out of choice, the concession does not apply. But a memo stating who is to work and until when is enough.

TIP

Avoid having a regular pattern to these payments. If you work late on the same day each week, then the Taxman says the concession does not apply.

TIP

If the number of journeys exceed 60, don't panic, you're not taxed on the full amount; if 70 journeys were made, then 60 payments would be tax-free and ten taxable.

TIP

It's not reasonable to use public transport if the level of availability/reliability of the service at that time of night is bad, resulting in the journey home being much longer than normal. So ask your employees to check out the timetables and prove this point in a note to you.

Warning. If, because of working late, you paid yourself the equivalent of, say, a train fare home, this would be taxable. Always pay yourself the equivalent of the taxi fare home.

Car sharing breaks down

If your spouse or partner who normally shares a car with you to get to work, has to go home early because of a domestic emergency, your company can pay the cost of their journey home. There will be no tax or NI to pay if the circumstances couldn't have been anticipated or planned for.

TIP

If you and your partner share a car to get to work, this means your company could pay for either of you to travel home by taxi. Just write "car share, domestic emergency" on the petty cash slip or expenses claim. But don't use this trick too often.

9.3.   PERSONAL TRAVEL

Personal travel as part of a business trip is normally only tax deductible where it actually reduces the cost of the business journey to the company, e.g. staying a Saturday night to take advantage of a lower cost airfare on a Sunday. Where additional non-business journey costs are incurred (e.g. staying on for a leisure weekend in the hotel) these must normally be met by the individual employee not the company, to avoid a tax problem for both. However, weekend accommodation can be reimbursed where the traveller is unable to return home as part of a longer business trip. Personal travel by its very nature can't be covered by a dispensation and so any such expenses will need to go on the individual's P11D.

9.3 1.   Travel with a spouse or partner

If a member of staff is accompanied by a spouse or partner who is not involved in company business, the Taxman expects the traveller to bear the cost. However, if there is a business reason for them to accompany the traveller, then their costs can be deductible for the company but assessed as a benefit-in-kind on the traveller.

9.4.   VAT

Many businesses automatically claim VAT on train, air and bus tickets and don't think about it until they get a visit from a VAT inspector. The problem is that passenger transport in a vehicle, ship or aircraft designed or adapted to carry not less than ten people (including the driver) is zero rated.

This means there is no VAT to be claimed and if the Taxman finds that you have been claiming VAT back, he will disallow it and charge you interest. However, he can only go back four years.

9.4.1.   Taxis

Taxi services are a taxable supply but most self-employed taxi drivers are not VAT registered, so when you get a receipt for your expenses claim, ask the taxi driver if he has charged VAT.

9.5.   DISPENSATION AVAILABLE?

Reimbursed travel expenses need to be disclosed on a P11D or covered by a dispensation. However, the Taxman will normally readily give a dispensation for "travel" covering the reimbursement of the costs actually incurred by employees, regardless of what form the transport takes (but excluding mileage allowances). The dispensation does not cover reimbursement of travel between an employee's home, or any other place that is not a workplace, and their normal place of work.

9.5.1. Travel expenses policy

Including a travel expenses policy in your staff handbook will provide evidence to the Taxman that you only reimburse qualifying travel expenses. This will make him more likely to grant a dispensation for these expenses, reducing the amount of work you need to do at the year-end. The policy should specifically make reference to home-to-office travel, which should not be included in business travel claims.

KEY POINTS

By land, sea or air
- if your job requires you to travel you can claim for the cost regardless of which form of transport you use. However, it must be a business not a private or commuting journey.

Late night taxis
- if, because of working late, you paid yourself the equivalent of, say, a train fare home, this would be taxable. Always pay yourself the equivalent of the taxi fare home.

VAT
- passenger transport in a vehicle, ship or aircraft designed or adapted to carry not less than ten people (including the driver) is zero rated. So don't try to claim VAT on the cost of these.

CHAPTER 10

UK subsistence

10.1. THE EXPENSE

The Taxman allows your company to reimburse a director/employee the actual cost of their business travel, including subsistence, such as meals. If an overnight stay is also needed, then the cost of the accommodation and any necessary meal is also part of business travel (see Chapter 12).

Subsistence includes costs incurred in the course of the journey and meals necessarily purchased whilst at a temporary workplace. The employee doesn't need to take into account the costs saved as a result of the business travel. For example, if a meal cost is claimed as part of the travel expenses, no deduction is required for the cost of that meal saved at home.

The claim for reimbursement should be supported by a receipt to avoid the company having a problem obtaining a Corporation Tax deduction for this expense. However, the reality is that maintaining complete and accurate documentation for all transactions is a practical impossibility. The Taxman has recognised this and recently revised his guidance on claiming reimbursement of employees' expenses by the use of "scale rates". Subsistence expenses are an ideal candidate for scale rate payments.

It's also worth noting that payments of incidental expenses connected with business travel (such as the purchase of newspapers) are normally allowable for tax purposes despite not being business expenditure. However, the Taxman sets maximum sums per night.

10.2. AGREEING A TAILORED SCALE RATE WITH THE TAXMAN

Where you have a number of employees who travel frequently, you can reduce the work involved in processing their expenses claims by imposing a scale rate payment to cover items such as hotels, meals etc. Set the scale rates at the average cost of each expense category, e.g. hotel room or evening meal, not at the maximum cost an employee may incur. The Taxman doesn't like the idea of employees making a profit out of expenses claims. Unless you have a concession in place that covers your scale rate payments, you will have to tax the amounts paid.

TIP

Write to the Taxman telling him what scale rates you plan to pay and what type of expenses those rates will cover. If the Taxman agrees, you can pay the scale rates without deduction of tax. You may have to provide a random sample of expenses claims, plus receipts. This is to prove that the scale paid represents what the employees are actually spending on allowable subsistence expenses. However, once the permission is granted you won't have to do the sampling exercise again, unless the circumstances under which you pay those scale rates change.

TIP

Pitch your scale rate at a fairly modest level which, on average, will be enough to cover the relevant expenses. This way you are more likely to get is approved by the Taxman.

Warning. Scale rate payments can only be paid when the employee has incurred an allowable expense. A scale rate payment which is paid irrespective of whether the employee has incurred an allowable expense is simply a taxable payment of earnings.

10.2.1. A 10% sample

The Taxman had proposed that expenses could be reimbursed without the need for the retention of detailed receipts by all employees if a sampling procedure were carried out whereby 10% of all employees (chosen at random) were selected and required to keep detailed records of expenses for a month and those expenses were then used to calculate the scale rate for employees in general. However, this approach was too complex to be workable, so the need for a comprehensive internal benchmarking exercise has been removed.

TIP

Adopt this 10% sample approach if your company is trying to justify a bespoke flat rate allowance with the Taxman.

10.3. BENCHMARK SCALE RATES

The Taxman has introduced a set of advisory benchmark scale rate payments. These are the maximum tax and NI-free amounts that can be paid if your company chooses to use the system. It can pay less than this rate if it wants to do so; however, any excess over the benchmark rate is subject to tax and NI.

The benchmark scale rates that have applied since April 6 2009:

Description	Amount (up to)
Breakfast rate	£5
One meal (five-hour) rate	£5
Two meal (ten-hour) rate	£10
Late evening meal rate	£15

10.3.1. What time is "breakfast" or "late evening"?

The breakfast rate applies where the employee has to leave home before 6.00am and incur a cost on a meal after the business journey has started.

The late evening meal rate applies where the employee has to work later than usual, finishes work after 8.00pm having worked their normal day and has to buy a meal (which they would normally have at home) before the return business journey ends.

Both of these rates are for use in exceptional circumstances only and are not intended for employees with regular early or late work patterns. So don't overdo the claim!

10.3.2. More than one meal a day?

Benchmark scale rate payments are limited to three meals on one day (24-hour period). A meal is defined as a combination of food and drink. For every five hours of business travelling you are entitled to claim for the cost of an actual meal taken. And, unlike the breakfast and late evening meals, the over five and ten-hour rates can be paid regardless of regularity.

10.3.3. Qualifying conditions

Benchmark scale rates must only be used where all the qualifying conditions are met. The rather straightforward (for the Taxman) conditions are that:

- the travel must be in the performance of an employee's duties or to a temporary place of work
- the employee should be absent from their normal place of work or home for a continuous period in excess of five or ten hours
- the employee should have incurred a cost on a meal (food and drink) after starting the journey.

10.3.4. Opting in

Your company can opt to use the benchmark rates by ticking the appropriate box on Form P11DX or by stating their intention to use them in a letter to the Taxman. The request may be part of a new dispensation application or a revision to an existing dispensation (see Chapter 6).

Compared to bespoke scale rates, your company will not have to undertake a sampling exercise before the dispensation can be agreed and granted. Similarly, if you were to seek a dispensation with scale rate payments that are lower than the benchmark rates, you would not have to undertake a sampling exercise.

10.3.5. Overnight subsistence

A benchmark rate has not been set for overnight subsistence. It will still be necessary to agree a rate, if applicable, with the Taxman (See Chapter 12).

10.4. PERSONAL INCIDENTAL EXPENSES

It's worth mentioning that payments of incidental expenses connected with business travel (such as the purchase of newspapers) are normally allowable for tax purposes despite not being business expenditure. However, the maximum sum which can be reimbursed for incidentals is only £5. Any expenditure in excess of this amount makes the whole payment (not the excess over the limit) taxable as income in the hands of the employee.

10.5. VAT

In order to recover any VAT, your company normally needs a VAT invoice. However, for the majority of subsistence claims the claimant will probably only be able to obtain a less detailed receipt. These are for supplies of less than £250 (excluding VAT) and have the supplier's VAT registration number on them.

> **TIP**
>
> There's no need to keep an invoice/receipt to claim back VAT if the cost of supply is less than £25.

10.6. DISPENSATION AVAILABLE?

All your company really has to do to apply for a dispensation to cover subsistence payments is tick the relevant box on the P11DX and send it to the Taxman (or apply by a separate letter). It should limit payments of travel or subsistence associated with business journeys to either:

- actual cost within the business's own set limit

- a bespoke scale rate agreed with the Taxman based on a sample of expense claims; or

- the Taxman's advisory benchmark scale rates.

The reasonable and necessary cost of a meal/snack and beverages incurred by an employee whilst undertaking a business journey is usually included in the section of a Dispensation Notice relating to travel (excluding mileage allowances).

Download Zone

For a **Sample Dispensation Notice**, visit **http://books.indicator.co.uk**. You'll find the access code on page 2 of this book.

KEY POINTS

Avoiding the Taxman's interest
- to deflect the Taxman's unwanted attention, limit payments of travel or subsistence associated with business journeys to either: **(1)** actual cost within the business's own set limit; or **(2)** a bespoke scale rate agreed with the Taxman based on a sample of expense claims; **(3)** the Taxman's own advisory benchmark scale rates.

Scale rates
- if your employees make frequent business trips, the expense claims they hand in on their return can be time consuming to process. Get the Taxman to agree to the scale rates you want to use in the UK by providing evidence of a random sample of expense claims, plus receipts. This should also confirm their tax deductibility for your company
- one of the core principles behind the use of a scale rate is that the expenditure must have occurred. So, for example, where a flat rate daily subsistence allowance is paid but the actual expenditure incurred is less than the allowance, this creates a tax liability on the employee.

UK subsistence

CHAPTER 11

Overseas travel and subsistence

11.1. INTRODUCTION

If your director's or employee's job requires them to travel outside the UK, i.e. overseas, they can claim for their travel expenses - but only for the cost of the journey - by land, sea or air. If they use their own car to make a trip to, say, mainland Europe, your company can make mileage allowance payments to cover their costs and there is no tax on this (see Chapters 7 and 8).

As well as transport, the cost of business travel includes subsistence, such as meals. For UK travel the Taxman allows employers to agree a subsistence scale rate with him (see Chapter 10). However, he reckons that most employers will not have enough internationally mobile employees to enable them to undertake a meaningful sampling exercise of their expenses to justify a bespoke scale rate. So for travelling outside the UK the Taxman has published benchmark costs (in local currencies) for accommodation and subsistence expenses. If your company uses these rates to reimburse directors/employees, there's no need for them to produce expenses receipts.

It's also worth noting that payments of incidental expenses connected with business travel, such as the purchase of newspapers, are normally allowable for tax purposes despite not being business expenditure. However, the Taxman sets a maximum sum of £10 per night outside the UK for this.

11.2. BENCHMARK RATES FOR ACCOMMODATION AND SUBSISTENCE

These benchmark rates are the maximum tax and NI-free amounts that can be paid if your company chooses to use this system. It can pay less than this rate if it wants to; however, any "allowance" over the benchmark rate is subject to tax and NI.

The Taxman's tables for accommodation and subsistence expenses include rates for: **(1)** hotel room per night; **(2)** subsistence rates per 24 hours, covering the cost of meals and travel to the customer or office; and **(3)** subsistence rates for five and ten-hour periods, where the employee is in the country for less than 24 hours but more than five or ten hours (see http://www.hmrc.gov.uk/manuals/eimanual/EIM05250.htm).

> **TIP**
>
> Where no benchmark costs are given, your company can pay your employees £4 per day plus the actual accommodation and meal costs incurred (supported by receipts).

Note. Whilst most rates are published in the local currency, or US dollars or euros, there are a number of countries where he has published a room rate in either dollars or euros but has the over five-hour, ten-hour and residual rates shown in the local currency.

TIP

Employers are not obliged to use the published rates. You can reimburse directors'/employees' actual expenses, or negotiate a scale rate amount which more accurately reflects their spending patterns.

TIP

The benchmark rates do not cover other expenses associated with the journey, such as the cost of a taxi to the airport in the UK, or necessary refreshments taken at the airport. These can be claimed for separately.

11.2.1. Meals provided by a host

If an individual receives free meals and accommodation, for example, if staying as the guest of another company, your company can still reimburse, per day, 10% of the appropriate total residual rate for that country **(EIM05255)**. Any meals that the employee still has to pay can be reimbursed using the full meal rate.

However, the "free meal" is also used to adjust the over five-hour, over ten-hour and total residual rates. For example, if an employee is provided with dinner on a particular day, the over five-hour, over ten-hour or total residual rates which would otherwise have been paid are reduced by the amount of the dinner rate for that location.

11.2.2. The Taxman's examples

To see how the Taxman's benchmark rates fit into an overall overseas business trip expense claim have a look at the examples he has provided on his website http://www.hmrc.gov.uk/manuals/eimanual/EIM05280.htm.

11.3. PERSONAL TRAVEL

Personal travel as part of a business trip is normally only tax deductible where it actually reduces the cost of the business journey to the company, e.g. staying a Saturday night to take advantage of a lower cost airfare on a Sunday. Where additional non-business journey costs are incurred, e.g. staying on for a leisure weekend in the hotel, these must normally be met by the individual employee not the company to avoid a tax problem for both. However, weekend accommodation can be reimbursed where the traveller is unable to return home as part of a longer business trip. Personal travel by its very nature can't be covered by a dispensation and so any such expenses will need to go on the individual's P11D.

11.3.1. Travel with a spouse or partner

If a member of staff is accompanied by a spouse or partner who is not involved in company business, the Taxman expects the traveller to bear the cost of their spouse/partner. However, if there is a business reason for a spouse or partner to accompany them, costs then incurred for the companion can be deductible for the company but will be assessed as a benefit-in-kind on the traveller.

11.4. INCIDENTAL EXPENSES

The actual cost of incidental expenses, such as personal telephone calls, newspapers, laundry, any necessary medication (such as malaria tablets) and bottled water can be claimed.

Note. If the total reimbursed for such incidental overnight expenses exceeds £10 a night, the total will be a taxable benefit.

11.5. PASSPORT AND VISA REQUIREMENTS

It's the traveller's responsibility to maintain a current passport with more than six months until the expiry date and to ensure that any visas required are obtained in advance of travel. The cost of visas can be recovered. Frequent travellers can claim for the cost of a second passport.

11.6. EXCHANGE RATES

Foreign currency transactions should preferably be claimed at the actual exchange rate incurred. Where a standard exchange rate is used, an additional claim may be made for any material difference between the default rate and the rate actually incurred on production of a copy of the bank or credit card statement.

11.7.   VAT

Many businesses automatically claim VAT back on train, air and bus tickets and never think about it until they get a visit from a VAT inspector. However, passenger transport in a vehicle, ship or aircraft designed or adapted to carry not less than ten people (including the driver) is zero rated.

That means there's no VAT to be claimed and if the inspector finds that you have been claiming VAT back, he will disallow it and charge you interest. However, he can only go back four years.

11.7.1.   VAT on EU expenses

Where your company incurs expenses in another EU state, e.g. hotel bills or goods not imported into the UK, unless it's registered for VAT in the country concerned, it can only claim back the foreign VAT by using the new cross-border electronic refund system. This was introduced in January 2011; claims must be submitted within nine months of the end of the calendar year in which the expense was incurred, e.g. for the year ended December 31 2010, the deadline is September 30 2011.

For more information on this refund procedure, see the Taxman's **Notice 723A** available from http://www.hmrc.gov.uk/.

Tɪᴘ

You can reclaim VAT on expenses incurred in other EU countries by using the cross-border electronic refund system.

11.8.   DISPENSATION AVAILABLE?

You don't need to include on Forms P11D payments for accommodation and subsistence at or below the published rates. However, if your company reimburses costs that exceed these rates, it must include them on the P11Ds unless it has a dispensation in place that covers overseas travel and subsistence (see Chapter 6).

11.8.1.   Overseas travel policy

Including an overseas travel expenses policy in your staff handbook will provide evidence to the Taxman that you only reimburse qualifying travel expenses. This will make him more likely to grant a dispensation for these expenses, reducing the amount of work you need to do at the year-end.

Download Zone

For an **Expenses Policy**, visit **http://books.indicator.co.uk**. You'll find the access code on page 2 of this book.

KEY POINTS

By land sea or air

- business travellers outside the UK can claim for the cost of that travel regardless of which form of transport they use. However, it must be a business not a private (or commuting) journey.

Benchmark scale rates

- the Taxman has introduced a set of benchmark scale rate payments for overseas accommodation and subsistence. If your company uses these rates to reimburse employees, there's no need for the employees to produce receipts
- where no benchmark subsistence costs are given, your company can pay £4 per day plus the actual accommodation and meal costs incurred (supported by receipts)
- you are not obliged to use the published rates. Instead, your company can reimburse directors'/employees' actual expenses, or even try to negotiate a scale rate amount which more accurately reflects the actual spending patterns.

Dispensation

- it's best to have a dispensation in place that covers overseas travel and subsistence, particularly if you intend to pay more than the Taxman's benchmark scale rates.

VAT

- passenger transport in a vehicle, ship or aircraft designed or adapted to carry not less than ten people (including the driver) is zero rated
- you can reclaim VAT on expenses incurred in other EU countries by using the cross-border electronic refund system.

CHAPTER 12

Hotels and other accommodation

12.1. THE EXPENSE

In general terms, the company can claim a full tax deduction for genuine business travel and for the cost of related hotel accommodation (and subsistence). It doesn't matter what class of hotel the director/employee stays in - a deluxe five star or a cheap and cheerful B&B. Just try to be consistent in the type of accommodation you choose or have a written company policy on acceptable accommodation for different levels of employee.

If necessarily away from base overnight, the company can reimburse the actual cost of relevant meals on presentation of receipts. Where appropriate, staff may dine in the hotel and claim the actual cost of a reasonable meal through their hotel bill. If certain meals have been provided for, such as breakfast included in the accommodation charge or location catering for lunch, only the other meals may be claimed.

For overseas travel the Taxman's benchmark rates can be used (see below).

12.2. INCIDENTAL EXPENDITURE

There is a relief for minor, personal incidental expenses added to a hotel bill. Items such as personal telephone calls, newspapers, laundry, and bottled water can be claimed if they are £5 or less per night (£10 if abroad, see Chapter 11); they don't need to be returned on P11Ds, and there won't be a tax or NI bill for you.

If the hotel room was booked personally by the director/employee, and your company is merely reimbursing the full cost, then those personal items will be liable to employees' NI. However, if your company had booked, i.e. contracted for the hotel room, then those items will not be liable to employees' NI. So make sure your company contracts for the hotel room even if the director/employee actually settles the bill.

If on a UK trip and the personal expenses are, for example, £3 for one night and £6 for the second night of a two-night stay, then there is no liability because the expenditure is considered on a stay-by-stay basis and so the average is below £5 per night.

Trap. The exemption is all or nothing. Firstly, the employee can't claim a tax deduction for expenditure that is not reimbursed by an employer. Secondly, if the limit is exceeded, then the whole amount is taxable, not just the excess.

A practical issue that might arise is where the incidental expenses of a number of different employees are shown together on one bill. If you are not careful a director's (heavier) share could end up averaged out amongst other employees. You are allowed to make a reasonable apportionment of the bill if the individual expenditure can't be easily identified.

Warning. The Taxman has gone on record saying that your company has to check that the amounts are not exceeded and that you don't accidentally reimburse the expenses twice - first as part of the hotel bill and a second via a separate expenses claim. So what should you do?

TIP

Have a clear company policy stating that any overpayments will be reimbursed to the company (before the next P11D is prepared). This would avoid a possible penalty for an incorrect completion of the P11D. Clearly, no P11D entry is required if the incidentals are within the permitted limits.

12.3. ACCOMMODATION FOR SPOUSE/PARTNER

Problems may arise with your travelling companion if they are there in a non-business capacity. Naturally, if another employee accompanies you on the trip their expenses will be deductible in the same way as yours. But if the employee is also your spouse, a tax inspector might become a little suspicious.

TIP

Make sure you have evidence to show why your spouse/employee is attending, e.g. minutes of meetings attended, a pass for the trade fair, etc.

If your spouse is not an employee, their attendance will not disqualify the business nature of the trip. However, if the company pays for the spouse, the director/employee has to pay tax - unless you can show that they attended to assist you with the trip. For example, if you visit a trade fair in, say, France, and your spouse is fluent in French, their costs could legitimately be claimed as those of an interpreter. The Taxman will need evidence of practical qualifications. They might even attend in a consultancy capacity, perhaps because they are skilled in marketing. You'd need to show membership of a recognised professional/trade body or a relevant sideline business.

Naturally, you should always keep receipts. However, if the hotel bill says something like *"Two nights' accommodation for two people at £79 per person per night"*, you won't be able to claim a deduction for the cost of your spouse's stay. Some business people choose hotels that charge for the room on a flat rate per night basis, irrespective of occupancy.

12.4. STAYING WITH FRIENDS

The cost of hotels can mount up very quickly if your work requires you to frequently travel on business. But what if your travels take you to the same parts of the country on a regular basis? You may have friends or family in the area you could stay with. Perhaps you could even cultivate a friend you could lodge with to your mutual tax advantage?

Assume you are staying with a friend and want to show your gratitude to your host by, say, paying for an evening meal or giving them some cash for their trouble. This leads to two questions: can you claim the cost of your gift against tax, and will your friend or relative end up with a tax bill as a result?

One option is to incorporate the idea of staying with friends within a company policy. That way it becomes a function of the business rather than just a personal decision. This is an important factor when claiming any business expense against tax.

> **TIP**
>
> Amend your company's policy to allow for payment of a reasonable overnight allowance to any employee/director who stays over necessarily with a friend or relative whilst on business.

The Taxman says that, *"It is not intended that this allowance should be similar in amount to the expense of staying in a hotel, nor that the allowance should necessarily meet the full cost of a meal for two."* A payment of up to £25 per night is considered to be reasonable, but this is only a guideline and in our view we would say it depends on where you were staying.

If the arrangement with your friend or family member is put on a more formal basis, they could charge you rent for occupation of the room. This could be greater than the £25 suggested by the Taxman, but obviously less than you would pay for your hotel. The "rent" receivable by your friend would be tax-free under the rent-a-room scheme, provided the amount they received from the activity was less than £4,250 in any tax year.

> **TIP**
>
> The friend can take money for providing food and hospitality. This can still be tax-free if it's within the rent-a-room limit.

Note. Rent for occupying the room should be declared as property income on a tax return. If, however, meals or other services, e.g. laundering, are provided, then the income is treated as a trade. Therefore, it must be declared on the trading income section of the tax return.

12.5. OVERSEAS TRIPS

For overseas travel you can use the Taxman's latest list of benchmark rates which shows how much can be paid tax and NI-free to a director or employee who travels abroad. The list shows, country by country, the amounts that are allowed for each type of expense, e.g. hotel, lunch, dinner etc., or you can pay a round sum to cover the lot (see http://www.hmrc.gov.uk/manuals/eimanual/EIM05250.htm).

TIP

The benchmark rates will give your employees scope to make some tax-free money by spending less than the benchmark amount.

EXAMPLE

Sundial Ltd sends two of its sales force to a trade fair in Geneva; they arrive at midday on Monday and catch a flight home early Thursday evening. The Company leaves it up to the employees to pay for everything except the flight which is settled direct with the airline. It pays each employee €1,123, about £985, to cover all food, accommodation and local travel costs. The employees manage their costs well and stay in a modest hotel. They actually only pay out £650 each meaning they walk away with £335 tax and NI-free.

12.6. VAT

Generally, you can reclaim VAT on hotel bills (including VAT on meals taken there). You can't reclaim VAT on hotel expenses when you pay an employee a flat rate. Neither can you reclaim VAT on any hotel accommodation that is for non-business use, such as a holiday tagged on to a business trip.

12.7. DISPENSATION FROM THE TAXMAN

When applying for a dispensation you'll be asked by the Taxman to confirm that you only pay for accommodation linked to business travel (see Chapter 6). Including a travel expenses policy for both the UK and overseas in your staff handbook will provide evidence to the Taxman that you only reimburse qualifying expenses. This will make him more likely to grant a dispensation for these expenses, reducing the amount of work you need to do at the year-end.

Download Zone

For an **Expenses Policy**, visit **http://books.indicator.co.uk**. You'll find the access code on page 2 of this book.

KEY POINTS

The expense

- there is a tax-free limit for incidental overnight expenses. Watch out for overpayments and have in place a clear company policy that any will be repaid by the employee
- if an overnight stay is needed then the cost of the accommodation and any necessary meals is part of the cost of business travel. If the overnight stay is in a hotel, claim the hotel bill including the meal cost.

Accommodation for spouse/partner

- you can only claim for your spouse if they attend, e.g., in a consultancy role
- book hotels that charge a flat rate per night rather than per person.

Staying with friends

- have a company policy that pays any employee/director a reasonable overnight allowance for expenses incurred staying with a friend or relative when on business. It will qualify for a tax deduction and could be tax-free for your friend.

Overseas trip

- for an overseas business trip your company can pay a benchmark scale rate tax-free instead of the actual costs. This will give the director/employee scope to make some tax-free money by spending less than the benchmark amount.

CHAPTER 13

Telephones

13.1. THE EXPENSE

Payments by employers that do no more than reimburse the actual cost of outgoing business calls are not regarded as earnings by the Taxman. So directors/employees can fill in an expenses claim for business calls made on either their landline at home or their private mobile phone. The Taxman would, however, expect an itemised bill to be attached.

Download Zone

For an **Expenses Claim Form**, visit **http://books.indicator.co.uk**. You'll find the access code on page 2 of this book.

Reimbursing the cost of phone cards for pay-as-you-go mobiles is regarded as income for the employee and liable to income tax and NI. So it's best to ban this under your company's expenses policy.

Business calls from a call box or hotel room can also be reimbursed through your expenses system. The employee just needs to separate them out from the hotel invoice.

Any line rental charge (either landline or mobile) can't be reimbursed without creating a tax liability for both the company and the employee. Again, a simple prohibition in your policy should avoid the problem.

13.2. DISPENSATION AVAILABLE?

To obtain a dispensation, you have to confirm on the online P11DX that all reimbursements that your company makes:

- relate to business calls (itemised bills available)
- do not include line rental
- do not include mobile phone contracts
- do not include equipment or phone packages.

Direct contract. You can claim a dispensation if you pay for a dedicated business line at the employee's home. However, this telephone cost comes under the benefit-in-kind legislation and won't be claimed through expenses. In that case don't be caught out by the Taxman's P11DX question which casually asks, *"Does the Company or the employee subscribe to the telephone line?"*

13.3. COMPANY POLICY

If you insert the following into your expenses policy, it should be acceptable to the Taxman:

"When you use your own home or mobile phone on Company business, the cost of itemised business calls will be met on production of an itemised bill. No rental charges will be paid by the Company, irrespective of whether these include a certain amount of free call time. HMRC will only allow the Company to reimburse business call costs.

The Company will not meet the cost of phone cards for pay-as-you-go mobiles.

If no itemised bill is available, a schedule of logged business calls should be attached. This will be acceptable provided the total is less than £......... (insert figure) per quarter.

The Company will meet the cost of business calls from a call box or hotel room, provided details of the call, including the length and to whom, are included on the expense claim.

The Company will not reimburse the cost of hands-free equipment or accessories."

13.4. VAT

If an invoice isn't made out to the VAT-registered person (i.e. your company), the company can't claim any VAT. Where there is no customer name on retail receipts that's OK, but it simply won't wash with any itemised phone bill which is clearly not in your company's name.

If a VAT receipt has been submitted, you can generally separate the VAT and claim it in the VAT account. The cost of calls is normally listed on the bill before VAT is added.

13.4.1. Call boxes and hotel rooms

> **TIP**
>
> There is no need to have an invoice/receipt to claim back VAT if the cost of supply is less than £25.

TIP

If the VAT included is not shown separately on a receipt, you can legitimately calculate and claim it as 1/6th (or 20/120) of the total amount. For example, a £12 payment includes VAT of £2.

KEY POINTS

Business calls only

- you can ask your company to reimburse you the cost of business calls made on your own phone(s) (landline or mobile), supported by itemised bills. Just highlight the items you want to claim for on the bill addressed to you
- if no itemised bill is available, attach a schedule of logged business calls.

Line rental

- line rental can't be reimbursed without creating a tax liability for both the employee and the company.

VAT

- your company shouldn't reimburse the VAT element of your employee's phone bill as it can't claim it back itself. The cost of calls is normally listed on the bill before VAT is added.

CHAPTER 14

Entertaining

14.1. THE EXPENSE

The cost of entertaining is not a deductible expense for tax purposes either for you or your company, so it's important to know what's classed as entertainment.

Business entertainment includes hospitality of any kind (for example, meals, parties, hospitality tents at sporting events) provided by you or a member of your staff, in connection with your business. It doesn't include anything provided for members of staff, except where the provision of entertainment for the staff is incidental to its provision for clients. This means that a staff party won't come under these rules, but a member of staff attending an event for clients will.

14.1.1 Customers

If you provide customers with free food, drinks, or tickets to, e.g. the rugby, the Taxman says you must exclude the full cost of the event from your accounts, so you don't get tax relief on anything that involves entertaining customers. However, here are four ways around the Taxman's strict rule that you can use for different occasions.

1. Give and take

Entertaining is essentially a one-sided bargain. The customer passively enjoys the hospitality, while you as the host pick up the bill. If the customer is obliged to give something in return for the hospitality, the event becomes a two-way business transaction and is not entertaining.

> EXAMPLE
>
> You ask customers to attend a seminar about your new product and to come armed with questions, during which you provide some glasses of wine. The customers accept the drinks as consideration for the time taken to attend and think up questions. You can deduct the cost of the wine and glass hire from your profits.

This works with gifts too.

> EXAMPLE
>
> If you give a customer a retail voucher in exchange for his used printer cartridges, which can be recycled, the customer is providing consideration in the form of the value of the empty cartridges. The voucher is not a gift as the value given by the customer is equal to the cost of the voucher.

2. Part of the trade

Where it is customary to provide complimentary refreshments as part of your normal business and the customers realise they are paying for this as part of the service, the cost of the free drinks is an allowable tax deduction.

EXAMPLE

Hair salons and car dealers frequently provide complimentary tea and coffee for customers and this cost is tax deductible.

3. Incidental cost

When the hospitality is minimal to the occasion no part of the total event expenses have to be disallowed. The Taxman doesn't define what he means by minimal. In his manual he gives examples of what can't be allowed so you can argue the point if challenged.

EXAMPLE

At a book launch there will normally be drinks and a cheese nibble or two provided for journalists, but the main aim of the event is to promote the book. If the cost of the cheese and wine is small compared to the total event, the cost of the sustenance is allowed.

4. Staff (within reason)

Entertaining your employees is tax deductible as long as it's not excessive. The Taxman also agrees that feeding non-employees who are directly involved in your business is allowable, so agency staff and self-employed contractors count towards the numbers involved in a staff meeting "over lunch".

However, the Taxman's generosity does not extend to the summer staff outing or Christmas dinner. On these occasions only current or retired staff of the company and their partners qualify, not future employees or self-employed contractors.

14.1.2. Entertaining yourself

During an enquiry the Taxman always expects to find some entertaining expenditure and looks closely at the nature of the expense incurred by the directors/employees. If, in reality, the money is being spent on entertaining personal friends, or otherwise social rather than business reasons, then the entertainment is fully taxable on the employee.

The same principles apply where a director/employee receives an allowance which is specifically intended to be spent on business entertaining. The company needs to disallow the expenditure in its computation and record the allowance on the

P11D. However, the director/employee can only avoid tax to the extent that the money was spent on genuine business entertaining.

In many instances, you will incur a particular expense which the business reimburses. In this case the payment the company makes will be specifically in respect of business entertaining costs and should be disallowed in the tax computations for the business.

You can then claim a tax deduction for this expenditure on business entertainment following the general principles for making such claims, meaning you don't pay any tax on what you have reimbursed them.

14.2. WHAT ARE THE POTENTIAL TAX SAVINGS?

If you pay for entertainment out of your own pocket, then it's likely that this comes out of income that has already suffered tax. If it's income from your company, this money has probably been extracted as either salary or dividends. If you can reduce your tax bill by getting the company to pay direct, then you are in a winning situation.

> EXAMPLE
>
> In a company the entertaining add-back for Corporation Tax (CT) is at, say, a CT rate of 20%. This produces additional tax of only £200 per £1,000 of entertaining spend. As a higher rate taxpayer, paying for entertainment out of dividends gives a tax cost of £250 per £1,000 and out of salary £580 per £1,000. The greater the difference between your effective rate of tax and the CT rate of your company, then the more tax you'll save by the company incurring the disallowable expenditure instead of you.

14.3. THE PAPERWORK

14.3.1. Contract with/invoice from the supplier

Where possible, get the invoices concerning entertainment costs to be contracted for and paid direct by your company. This avoids the reimbursed expenses hassle with P11Ds, etc.

14.3.2. On the VAT return

Your company can't claim VAT back on the purely entertaining element of any invoice. But it can apportion an invoice between, say, entertaining and subsistence and claim back the VAT on the latter.

Remember, gifts are not business entertainment, which means you can claim the input VAT back on them, provided they are less than £50 each (excluding VAT).

TIP

Don't forget, as a VAT registered trader your company can go back three years to claim VAT you incur on its gifts if it hasn't done so already.

EXAMPLE

Catherine ran a successful marketing business and each year sent her valued customers a nice bottle of wine or port valued at between £20 and £30. A few years ago she wanted to know if she could claim the VAT back on their purchase so she entered "wine" into the search engine on the VATman's website and it came back with the answer "business entertainment", on which the recovery of input VAT is blocked.

However, other rules allow the recovery of VAT on the purchase of business gifts. The even better news is that no output VAT is due when you give them away, provided the total value of business gifts to each recipient does not exceed £50 (excluding VAT) in any twelve-month period. Obviously the VATman expects you to choose the perfect "phrase" when using his search engine - in this case "business gifts" not "wine".

So Catherine could claim all the VAT back on her business gifts over the past three years and there was no output tax to pay. Her reclaim through her VAT return ended up at nearly £2,000.

14.3.3. On your P11D

In the absence of a dispensation on your P11D your company has to indicate whether or not the cost of any reimbursed entertaining will be disallowed in its tax computations. So in the Expense Payments section of the P11D (Section O) sub-heading Entertainment, don't just record the reimbursed expenses amount, tick the box too (just in front of it). Otherwise, the Taxman will assume the amount is taxable on you.

These special rules relating to entertaining expenses apply to all employees, not just those with P11Ds. Where appropriate, record these reimbursed expenses on P9Ds (at heading A1 Expenses Payments).

14.3.4. Dispensation available?

If you reimburse business entertaining expenses, you can claim a dispensation as long as the costs exclude entertaining of relatives, partners or shareholders. But this will only cover the following:

"The cost of entertaining customers, potential customers, suppliers or other business connections at genuine business occasions."

The following can usually be regarded as reasonable and genuine business occasions:

- product launches
- lunches and similar events for customers or potential customers at which business is discussed
- exhibitions and similar events at which products are on display for customers.

Claims for entertaining expenses should be supported with records of the amount spent on a particular occasion, the nature of the entertainment, the persons entertained and the reasons for the entertainment.

14.3.5. In the company's accounts

It may seem obvious but book entertainment costs to "entertaining".

The total "entertaining" figure per your company's accounts (from the detailed profit and loss account) needs to be added back to your company's profits in its Corporation Tax computation.

14.3.6. Your tax return

You simply take the figure given to you by the company on your P11D for "entertainment payments" and put this on your tax return. Then record a counter claim (within the same employment pages) that these were incurred by reason of your employment.

14.4. LOW, MEDIUM AND HIGH-RISK STRATEGIES

14.4.1. Low-risk

By being imaginative you can use the Taxman's own Business Income Manual against him. As a rule of thumb, entertainment costs which are customary to your trade or incidental to an event should be allowable.

Remember to tick the box on the P11D to confirm that entertaining expenses will be disallowed in the business's tax computation. Otherwise the Taxman can assume these are fully taxable on you.

If you get the paperwork right, the low-risk strategy is the one outlined above.

14.4.2. Medium-risk

You get assessed personally for entertainment payments as if they were income, because the Taxman doesn't accept that the expense is "wholly and exclusively" for the purpose of the company's trade. This would be the case if facts showed that the rationale behind incurring the expense is found to be personal not business, during an enquiry.

14.4.3. High-risk

If, in reality, company money is being spent on entertaining personal friends, or otherwise for social rather than business reasons, then the entertainment is fully taxable on you. The Taxman can go back up to six years to work out how much NI and tax is owed if he discovers you have been doing this. With interest on top, this could mean the company ends up facing quite a bill.

KEY POINTS

- the cost of entertaining is not a deductible expense
- if you provide customers with food, tickets, etc., the Taxman says you must exclude the full cost of the event from your accounts. However, there are four ways to get around this rule
- where possible, get the invoices concerning entertainment costs to be contracted for and paid direct by your company.

CHAPTER 15

Computer consumables

15.1. THE EXPENSE

Computer consumables include memory media such as disks, DVDs and USB sticks. Also associated with computers is the use of a printer which has its own consumables of paper and ink cartridges. Your company would normally provide such consumables at its premises and think no more of it. But what about employees who work at home or travel on business, buy consumables and then seek reimbursement from the company?

15.2. DISPENSATION AVAILABLE?

No dispensation; however, there is a tax exemption. If your company provides stationery and other consumables on its premises to enable an employee to perform their duties of employment, it has no reporting requirements and no tax or NI to pay.

There is also no tax charge on the expense that an employer incurs in providing directors and employees with supplies and services that:

- are provided other than on the employer's premises, e.g. employees who work at home or whilst travelling

- enable the director/employee to perform their duties of the employment, and any use for private purposes is not significant.

For example, if you have a company procedure that requires everyone to back up their data daily, then this is a duty of employment for which the individual needs computer memory media.

This exemption (s.316 of the **Income Tax and Pensions Act 2003**) can cover the provision of supplies and services such as: *"stationery and normal office or workshop materials and supplies"*. So if you would have supplied the computer consumable at the office, then you can provide it if the employee is travelling or working at home.

15.3. VAT

As a general rule, if an invoice isn't made out to the VAT-registered person, i.e. your company, then they can't claim back any VAT included on that invoice. Where a member of staff is claiming something back, and a less detailed VAT receipt has been submitted, you can generally claim the VAT if there is no customer name.

TIP

If the VAT included is not shown separately on a receipt, you can legitimately calculate and claim it as 1/6th (or 20/120) of the total amount.

EXAMPLE

Rory works form home travelling from there to various customers in his sales area. He uses his own printer to run off quotes, proposals, letters and marketing material. The latter is normally in colour. Each month he replaces both the black ink and colour cartridges for his printer. Sourcing from the cheapest high street retail outlet he only has a till receipt to back up his expenses claim to be reimbursed for the cost of the cartridges. This month he claimed £54 (2 x £27.00) for an ink cartridge on his expenses claim form and attached the till receipt.

Via the expenses claim his company can claim back input VAT of £54 x 20/120 = £9.00.

KEY POINTS

Exemption not dispensation

- if the computer consumable (including memory media) is provided for the sole purpose of enabling the director/employee to perform their duties of employment, there are no reporting or tax requirements to comply with
- the rule of thumb is that if you would have supplied the computer consumable at the office, then you can provide it if the employee is travelling or working at home.

Private use

- Private use of computer memory media is allowed, provided it isn't significant.

VAT

- if the VAT included is not shown separately on a receipt, you can legitimately calculate and claim it as 1/6th (or 20/120) of the total amount.

CHAPTER 16

Working from home

16.1. INTRODUCTION

The Taxman envisages the business situation where your Company has one or more directors/employees who have to work from home because either: **(1)** the facilities they need for their work aren't available at the workplace; **(2)** their work requires them to live too far from the workplace for it to be reasonable for them to travel there on a daily basis. If by doing so they incur additional household expenses, such as gas or electricity charges, your company is allowed to reimburse them for this. But how much can they claim without any tax implications for either of you?

16.2. THE £3 PER WEEK ALLOWANCE

For payments of up to £3 per week, your company doesn't need any records of the household expenses it's reimbursing.

> **TIP**
>
> It's possible to pay this allowance regularly through the company's payroll. Just make sure that it's flagged as non-taxable and non-NI able "other pay" or "expenses". This saves you having to remember to pay the allowance separately.

16.3. MATCHING ADDITIONAL EXPENDITURE

For amounts paid above £3 per week (£156 p.a.) your company needs documentation to show that the payment being made to the director/employee is no more than the additional household expenses they've incurred. Provided the amount you reimburse doesn't exceed this, your company has no reporting requirements or tax or NI to pay.

Warning. If the amount the company pays exceeds the employee's additional expenses, then it counts as earnings, and it's expected to apply PAYE tax and Class 1 NI on the excess via the payroll.

16.4. BROADBAND CONNECTION

The employee/director could claim the cost of a broadband connection if this were truly an additional cost of homeworking. However, the Taxman assumes that most people will have such a connection already for private purposes.

16

If the director/employee decides to install broadband at home themselves, no costs can be claimed. Instead, as part of homeworking arrangements, get the company to arrange for the installation of a separate business telephone line with broadband service solely for business use. This must be arranged, contracted and paid for direct by the company.

16.5. VOLUNTEERING TO WORK FROM HOME

An employee/director can also volunteer to work at home on a regular basis under a formal homeworking arrangement with their employer (your company). They don't have to work at home every day but there needs to be a regular pattern to this - for example, two days at home and three days in the office each week. The work they do at home should be an extension of what they normally do for the company.

Trap. If the company doesn't contribute, the director/employee can't claim relief separately for their expenses of working at home.

TIP

Make sure the company has a homeworking agreement in place between it and its employees/directors to allow it to pay them expenses tax and NI-free if they regularly work from home.

16.6. DISPENSATION AVAILABLE?

No dispensation is available because there is a tax exemption in place instead.

16.7. VAT

There is no input VAT to be claimed on the weekly allowance (either at the £3 a week or higher rate). However, the individual can include the VAT they are charged on the extra gas, electricity etc. used when calculating a higher rate than £3 per week.

16.7.1. VAT on broadband connection

If the company arranges for the installation of a separate business telephone line with broadband service (solely for business use), it can claim back any VAT it's charged by the supplier, either on the initial installation or the on-going subscription fees. However, this facility must be arranged, contracted and paid for directly by the company.

KEY POINTS

Weekly allowance
- an employee/director can volunteer to work at home on a regular basis under a formal homeworking arrangement with their employer (your company). There needs to be a regular patten to this work
- for homeworking expenses payments up to £3 per week, you don't need to provide any records. For amounts above this figure, you need supporting evidence to show the payment is no more than the additional household expenses they've incurred
- pay this through the payroll not via an expenses claim.

Broadband connection
- if the director/employee decides to install broadband at home themselves, no costs can be claimed, so arrange for the installation of a separate business telephone line with broadband service solely for business use. This must be arranged, contracted and paid for directly by the company.

VAT
- there is no input VAT to be claimed on a weekly expenses allowance. However, when calculating a higher rate, VAT can be included on the extra gas, electricity etc. used.

CHAPTER 17

Miscellaneous expenses

17.1. THE EXPENSE

With any expenses claim form there is usually a column at the end headed *"Other"* or *"Miscellaneous"*. Some entries dropped into this column often have a particular tax treatment that you ought to be aware of.

Download Zone

For an **Expenses Claim Form**, visit **http://books.indicator.co.uk**. You'll find the access code on page 2 of this book.

17.2. OFFICE SUPPLIES

Every office requires supplies to maintain its smooth operation and these might be conveniently grouped under the headings:

- catering - tea, coffee, other beverages etc.
- safety and security - keys being cut, batteries for the smoke alarms etc.
- janitorial - cleaning materials, soap dispensers for the hand basins, paper hand towels etc.

17.2.1. VAT on office supplies

Where a member of staff submits a claim, if a VAT receipt has been attached, you can generally separate out the input VAT and claim it back.

TIP

Tea, coffee etc. are zero rated if purchased from a shop. The other office supplies should have standard rate VAT included in their price.

TIP

There is no need to keep an invoice/receipt to claim back VAT if the cost of supply is less than £25.

TIP

If the VAT included is not shown separately on a receipt, you can legitimately calculate and claim it as 1/6th (or 20/120) of the total amount. For example, a £25 payment includes VAT of £4.16.

17.3. SUBSCRIPTIONS TO PROFESSIONAL ORGANISATIONS

Your company can claim a tax deduction for reimbursing directors/employees for fees and subscriptions they have paid to professional bodies if those bodies have been approved by the Taxman, see http://www.hmrc.gov.uk/list3/index.htm.

However, without a dispensation from the Taxman any reimbursement or direct payment has to be reported as a benefit-in-kind for the individual concerned, with income tax to be paid and employers' NI by the company.

Warning. If the professional body isn't approved, then your company is expected to deduct and pay PAYE tax and Class 1 NI on the amount.

17.3.1. Obtaining a dispensation

A dispensation can easily be obtained (see Chapter 6). The Dispensation Notice should read:

"Professional fees and subscriptions paid by or on behalf of an employee to an organisation, included in HMRC List 3, where the activities of the organisation are relevant to the office of employment in accordance with ss.343 and 344 of the **Income Tax (Earnings and Pensions Act) 2003.**"

Note. Professional fees and subscriptions are normally exempt from VAT, so there is no input VAT for your company to claim back on this expense.

17.4. INTEREST AND OTHER COSTS ON A PERSONAL CREDIT CARD

The Taxman regards the director/employee as responsible for interest and charges due to late payments of the balance on their credit or charge card.

TIP

However, if they submitted a correctly completed expenses claim in sufficient time and payment was subsequently delayed through no fault of their own, causing them to incur interest, they could legitimately submit a claim for compensation - equal to the relevant charges - to your company.

17.4.1. Cash advance handling fee

> **TIP**
>
> Where the employee/director needs to pay for business items in cash, they can withdraw it using their own credit or charge card. They can then claim the cost of the cash advance handling fee charged by the card provider as a necessary business expense. Of course, they must attach a copy of the statement to their claim and state why the cash was required.

Note. Credit card charges and interest are both exempt from VAT.

17.5. EYE TESTS AND GLASSES

Employers are required by law to provide, or meet the cost of, eye care tests and/ or corrective glasses for display screen equipment (DSE) use for their employees. The Taxman would not normally expect to levy a tax charge on this benefit-in-kind (s.266 of the Income Tax (Earnings and Pensions) Act). If the director/employee uses DSE as part of their work for more than two hours each day, they can apply for an eyesight test and the company can reimburse them for this. Where the eye examination shows that glasses are needed specifically for DSE work, the company can contribute to the cost of these too.

> **TIP**
>
> The director/employee can claim back the actual cost of the sight test and glasses, where applicable; to do this they should attach their receipt. Health and safety legislation considers an eye test to be an expense incurred in relation to employment.

17.6. DISPENSATION AVAILABLE?

You might be able to claim a dispensation for other "business only" expenses. Just provide the Taxman with details of the additional expenses you wish to include.

> **TIP**
>
> The online dispensation application Form P11DX has a box for this. However, it only has space for 2,000 characters. So if you need more room, make a manual application and attach a separate piece of paper.

Miscellaneous expenses

Office supplies

- tea, coffee etc. are zero rated if purchased from a shop. The other office supplies should have standard rate VAT included in their price. If purchased from an office supply company, the relevant VAT should be identified on their invoice

- there's no need to have an invoice/receipt to claim back VAT if the cost of supply is less than £25.

Subscriptions to professional organisations

- your company can obtain a tax deduction for reimbursing directors/ employees fees and subscriptions to professional bodies approved by the Taxman. However, it will need a dispensation to be able to leave these out of the reporting system.

Interest and other costs on a personal credit card

- if the payment of a correctly completed expenses claim is delayed causing the director/employee to incur interest on their personal credit card, they can be reimbursed the relevant charges.

- the director/employee can also claim the cost of a cash advance handling fee charged by their card provider if expenses had to be paid in cash.

Eye tests and glasses

- health and safety legislation considers an eye test to be an expense necessarily incurred in relation to employment.

CHAPTER 18

Cash advances

18.1. CASH EXPENSES

The majority of business expenses are easy to account for. This is because they either have an invoice attached or are purchased with a company credit card. With cash expenses however, there is often no convenient paperwork to indicate where the money might have gone. The use of debit and credit cards may be rapidly replacing and eliminating cash transactions, but there are still several types of minor expense that are more conveniently paid for with cash. These could include postage, office supplies, minor repairs, tips, petrol, parking and tolls, and public transport fares, among others.

If someone takes cash out of the company float, perhaps to cover any unforeseen expenses on a trip to see a client, then, in the absence of any evidence to the contrary, the Taxman might choose to regard the payment as extra income. That means having to pay tax on the money.

It is important, therefore, to secure concrete proof of any cash expenses. Tickets, receipts and bills will show that the money went on legitimate business purchases and not into someone's pocket. Of course, it is not always possible to get a receipt or a bill. In these cases, you ought to make sure that anyone who takes cash out should, on their return, put down on paper exactly how it was spent.

The record needs to be accurate and reasonably comprehensive. If the money was used on a visit to a client, it would help to record who the meeting was with, when it happened and why it was held. This way, it's easier to demonstrate that it was a genuine business expense and, therefore, tax deductible.

18.2. TAXMAN'S VIEW

The Taxman doesn't like cash because it doesn't give him a nice audit trail to follow. He just assumes that you are up to no good if cash is involved. OK, most business expenses these days are invoiced or settled using a company credit card, but cash floats are still used on certain occasions.

For example, you could be off to see a customer and you will need to meet out-of-pocket expenses. Naturally you take some cash from the petty cash tin, perhaps leaving a note to say how much was taken. In the absence of evidence, the Taxman will see the money as taken "net of tax". Meaning he wants to gross up the petty cash difference for income tax and NI and he will ask you to pay it.

EXAMPLE

Paul takes £100 per week from petty cash, a total of £5,200 for the year. He is a 40% taxpayer already paying employees' NI at 2%. £5,200 translates into £8,966 (£5,200/58%) gross salary. This means that the Taxman collects the difference of £3,766 plus £1,237 in employers' NI, making a total of £5,003. Hardly worth drawing the cash in the first place is it? Or, Paul has to draw dividend from his company to repay the £5,200 before the tax year closes, which will cost him an additional £1,300 (£5,200 x 25%) in income tax. A cheaper solution but it's still painful.

In practice, you might not be able to get receipts for everything you spend the cash on, e.g. street parking, or just forget to. A large cup of designer coffee in a railway station could cost you as much as £3.50. But who would remember to keep the receipt for this? If the Taxman sees you haven't got one, he would still want to tax you on the difference one way or another.

What you need to do is to collect evidence that the missing cost was a business expense. So when returning from your trip try and tie up where the money went. The important thing is to get the record as close as you can.

You could keep a record of where you travelled to, who you saw and what you spent in your diary. However, you probably don't feel comfortable with the Taxman nosing through your appointments etc. Better to record this on a separate sheet of paper, to which you can add a list of expenses matching what's been spent.

18.3. ADVANCES FOR EXPENSES

An advance on account of expenses to be incurred by an employee is strictly a loan for tax purposes. If the total of all loans from your company exceeds £5,000, then you pay tax on a notional interest benefit, calculated at a rate of 4%. However, the Taxman has issued a statement of practice which removes certain advances from this test. The main conditions that need to be satisfied are: **(1)** the maximum amount advanced at any one time must not exceed £1,000; **(2)** advances must be spent within six months; and **(3)** the employee must account for how they have spent the amount advanced. As long as these conditions are met such advances will not be treated as loans.

18.4. EUROS

From time-to-time a director or employee will have occasion to travel to Euroland on business. Most of the travel and subsistence can be taken care of by the company credit card. However, there is always the need to carry cash "just in case". Indeed, cash is a necessity for paying local taxes in some of the member sates. So you have a business need for a reasonable stock of Euros in the same way as you have a need for a petty cash float.

TIP

There is a good argument these days for having a Euro as well as a Sterling petty cash tin. If you personally need to dip into the Euro tin, remember to replenish it as soon as possible.

18.5. THE PAPERWORK

By taking the following steps you will be making sure that there is no room for a challenge by the Taxman. And with all the paperwork completed correctly there should be no risk of penalties arising at a later date either.

18.5.1. Your expense claim

Fill out an expenses claim. If you have spent some of the money on personal items, then record it as such. It's better to pay tax on the small amount taken rather than on the whole cash difference.

Download Zone

For an **Expenses Claim Form**, visit **http://books.indicator.co.uk**. You'll find the access code on page 2 of this book.

TIP

Have a pad of petty cash vouchers or post-it notes in your briefcase. Use these to note down a variety of minor expenses.

18.5.2. Company policy on overpayments

Key point. To help slow the Taxman down on "the difference is additional net salary" line of attack, make sure that the following appears in your company's expenses policy:

"Overpayments remain Company money at all times. They never form part of employees' salary or remuneration packages."

This also gives you the option of making good any overpayments (such as cash differences) within a reasonable period of them being discovered.

18.5.3. On the VAT return

In order to recover the VAT you are charged you should obtain a VAT invoice, although for supplies of less than £250 excluding VAT you need a less detailed tax invoice. Valid VAT receipts (with a VAT number) are required to claim back VAT on your expenses. However, by concession, there are some minor items that you don't need to have a receipt for. The supply of taxi services is a taxable supply but most self-employed taxi drivers are not VAT registered, so when you get a receipt for your expenses claim ask the taxi driver if they have charged VAT.

18.5.4. On your P11D

These are not reimbursed expenses so they don't need to be disclosed on your P11D or covered by a dispensation from the Taxman.

18.5.5. In the company's accounts

Any remaining petty cash differences from your cash withdrawals will be booked by your accountant as a reduction to your director's loan account, to be cleared by additional salary or dividend before the accounts are signed off for that year.

18.5.6. Your tax return

No additional entries are required. This should all have been taken care of through the other entries on your return.

18.6. LOW, MEDIUM AND HIGH-RISK STRATEGIES

18.6.1. Low-risk

If you get the paperwork right, the low-risk strategy is the one outlined above.

18.6.2. Medium-risk

The company does not get a tax deduction for your missing expenses because the Taxman doesn't accept that these expenses were "wholly and exclusively" for the purpose of the company's trade.

In the absence of expense claims the Taxman will be happy to include any unresolved petty cash differences as net salary from your company.

18.6.3. High-risk

You do nothing about your petty cash differences.

However, you won't have to wait for an enquiry before you have to deal with this, your accountant will have to make a decision about this "cash difference" when preparing your accounts or P11Ds.

> **KEY POINTS**
>
> - it's important to secure concrete proof of any cash expenses - the record needs to be accurate and reasonably comprehensive
> - if you don't have receipts, record a list of expenses.

CHAPTER 19

Maximising VAT recovery

19.1. INTRODUCTION

Expenses that your business reimburses to employees, such as motor fuel costs (including the fuel proportion of mileage allowances), parking and toll charges and subsistence payments, are all likely to include VAT. If your company is registered for VAT, it can generally offset any VAT its suppliers have charged it (input VAT) against any VAT it in turn is charging its customers (output VAT). This offset is given by putting a figure in the inputs box on your company's VAT return.

You are required to have a "valid tax invoice". If any of the stipulated information is missing it's not a valid invoice and you have no legal right to reclaim the input VAT. Sometimes obtaining a detailed invoice can be time consuming. However, the VATman has introduced some concessions in response to the problems of obtaining a detailed tax invoice in certain circumstances.

Some businesses automatically claim VAT back on all expenses and don't think about it until they get a visit from a VAT officer. The problem is that not all expenses include VAT and for expenses such as entertaining you are blocked from recovering the VAT anyway.

19.2. VALID VAT RECEIPTS

It makes practical sense to have your company's expenses claim form designed in such a way as to ensure that the claimant supplies all the information needed to process the expense claim quickly and accurately.

TIP

As a director/employee enter the gross amounts including VAT on your expenses claim form. Leave the VAT reclaim to your company's accountant. However, to make their job easier make sure you have a valid VAT receipt for expenditure you are claiming.

19.2.1. What is a valid VAT receipt?

A valid VAT receipt includes:

- the name and address of the supplier
- their VAT registration number
- the date of the purchase
- details of what goods or services have been purchased; and
- the VAT inclusive value of those goods or services in sterling.

Note. A VAT registration number consists of nine digits and is set out in the following format: 123 4567 89.

In order to recover the VAT you are charged you should obtain a VAT invoice, although for supplies of less than £250 (excluding VAT) you need only a "less detailed" tax invoice.

If the VAT included is not shown, you can legitimately calculate and claim it as 1/6th (or 20/120) of the total amount. For example, a £12 payment includes VAT of £2.

It's best if original receipts accompany all claims. Credit card slips or statements will not generally be accepted by the Taxman as evidence of business expenditure.

Warning. There is no VAT to be reclaimed where a scale rate for expenses is paid.

19.2.2. No receipts at all?

What if you don't have a nicely printed invoice, just a scrawled petty cash voucher, a receipt with a vague description of the expense or, worse still, nothing at all? Is there any hope of claiming the VAT back? The good news is "yes", subject to certain conditions being met.

Is a claim worth the effort? Yes. If, say, ten employees have each spent £10 per week on parking over the last year, then the VAT paid in total will be in excess of £860 (£5,200 x 20/120). That's easy money to claim and if your company missed out on that, what else is passing it by?

The following expenses don't require a receipt at all but they are limited to costs of less than £25 (inclusive of VAT) per transaction: **(1)** coin-operated machines; **(2)** car parking (but not at meters); **(3)** toll charges; and **(4)** telephone calls (from coin-operated call boxes).

Unless you have a receipt or invoice, you may only claim the VAT if you have properly recorded the expense. So make sure you, and your employees, itemise the cost in question on your expenses claim and that your bookkeeper is aware that they carry VAT.

19.2.3. Who are your employees for VAT?

Your company can only reclaim VAT on expenses reimbursed to its employees. Apart from a person directly employed by it; the following are included:

- directors, partners or anyone else that is managing the business
- self-employed people - subsistence expenses only - who are treated as normal employees
- helpers, stewards or other people essential to the running of an event.

A small group of people are <u>not</u> considered to be employees for reclaiming VAT on expense claim purposes:

- shareholders who are not also employees
- pensioners and former employees
- job applicants and interviewees.

19.3.   THE VAT RISK

Not all expenses include VAT and with some, such as entertaining, you are blocked from recovering any VAT you have been legitimately charged. This means that if a VAT officer finds that you have been claiming VAT back when you shouldn't have, he will ask for it back plus interest and penalties. However, he can only go back four years.

Examples of items on which you can't claim VAT back even if you have been charged it are:

- business entertainment
- goods bought under one of the second-hand schemes
- purchases for personal or private use
- purchases for non-business activities
- private accommodation for directors (but not hotel accommodation when away on business).

Examples of items on which no VAT is actually charged in the first place include:

- books and technical manuals
- insurance
- train, bus and airfares
- Royal Mail postage
- takeaway food.

The above lists are not comprehensive but should give you a reasonable idea of what to be aware of. However, there are some areas where you can maximise your input VAT claim.

19.3.1. Online help from the VATman

The webpage "What you can and can't reclaim VAT on?" (http://www.hmrc.gov.uk/vat/managing/reclaiming/reclaim.htm) is a helpful guide which attempts to explain when you can and can't reclaim VAT. The most relevant sections for reimbursement of expenses are:

- business entertainment, business gifts and benefits
- cars and motoring expenses: reclaiming VAT; and
- travel and subsistence: when you can reclaim VAT.

19.4. EXAMPLES OF NOTE

19.4.1. Subsistence

Although the VAT rules normally prevent your company from reclaiming VAT on supplies that are not made directly to it, there are certain circumstances where the rules are relaxed. For instance, the VAT element of subsistence expenses paid to directors/employees may be treated as input tax. In order to qualify for this concession, employees must be reimbursed for their actual expenditure and not merely receive round sum allowances. VAT invoices (which may be made out to the employee) must also be obtained. Receipts for subsistence whilst travelling, made out to an employee rather than the business, are therefore acceptable.

But what about a quick lunch with a contact, isn't that business entertainment? The answer is partly entertainment and partly subsistence. The main purpose of the meeting was business, entertainment was secondary. Therefore, the VAT on the subsistence relating to you can be recovered.

The VATman will allow you to reclaim a proportion of the total VAT on a bill. He will not insist that you identify who had what starter and main course. (The VATman admits to this point in **Notice 700/65/96, pars 2-5**.)

19.4.2. Tickets

Passenger transport in a vehicle, ship or aircraft designed or adapted to carry not less than ten people (including the driver) is zero rated. This means there is no VAT to be claimed and so you don't need a VAT receipt per se.

19.4.3. Reimbursement for road fuel

You are permitted to treat road fuel as your own supply which is purchased by a non-taxable person whom you then pay for the actual cost of the fuel. This would therefore allow you to recover input tax when you reimburse your employees for the cost of road fuel used in carrying out their employment duties. However, VAT invoices must be obtained to match the value of the fuel.

19.4.4. Mileage allowances

Your company can reclaim the VAT element (or a reasonable approximation) on the amount attributable to fuel of mileage allowances paid to directors/employees (or sub-contractors). The fuel element must be close to the fuel-only mileage rates published by the Taxman who also requires the following records to be kept:

- the mileage travelled and whether business or private
- the vehicle's engine size (cc)
- rate of mileage allowance
- the amount of input tax claimed.

The company must also have VAT receipts which total up to the amount on which VAT is being reclaimed in that VAT period.

19.4.5. Parking

You might not need a valid VAT invoice for off-street parking. A receipt with their VAT registration number is sufficient for amounts less than £25.

19.4.6. Taxis

The supply of taxi services is taxable but most self-employed taxi drivers are not VAT registered, so when you obtain a receipt for your expenses claim, ask the taxi driver if he has charged VAT. Plus, don't forget to claim for the tip you gave.

19.5. IN YOUR EXPENSES POLICY

Organisations lose thousands of pounds each year through unclaimed VAT associated with employee expenses claims. When your directors/employees are out of the office or working from home, you may well incur business expenses, e.g. parking, telephone, Internet charges etc., and these costs will often include VAT. So if you're not claiming the VAT back, you will be losing out. How do you tackle this?

> **TIP**
>
> Generally, when employees make an expenses claim the last thing they consider is obtaining a VAT receipt. So recovering this lost revenue means strict guidelines in your expenses policy, communication to directors/employees and having a VAT knowledgeable finance team in place.

Download Zone

For an **Expenses Policy**, visit **http://books.indicator.co.uk**. You'll find the access code on page 2 of this book.

19.6. VAT ON EU EXPENSES

If you conduct business overseas, your company can claim VAT back on many of the expenses incurred during the trip. Those that are eligible include:

- car rental
- hotels and accommodation
- information office expenses
- marketing costs
- petrol/diesel
- public transport (including buses, trains and taxis)
- restaurants and entertainment
- telephone bills.

19.6.1. EU automated claim system

Where your company incurs expenses in another EU state, e.g. hotel bills or goods not imported into the UK, unless it's registered for VAT in the country concerned, it can only claim back the foreign VAT by using the new cross-border electronic refund system. This was introduced in January 2011 and claims must be submitted within nine months of the end of the calendar year in which the expense was incurred, e.g. for the year ended December 31 2010, the deadline is September 30 2011.

For more information on this refund procedure see the Taxman's **Notice 723**A, available from http://www.hmrc.gov.uk.

19.7. FREELANCER'S EXPENSES

Does your company use self-employed staff/contractors? If it does, what happens to VAT on, say, their overnight expenses?

19.7.1. Subsistence

If they are VAT registered, it shouldn't pose much of a problem. They include their subsistence and other similar expenses as part of their component costs to you, charge VAT on the whole amount and you claim it all back on your VAT return.

19.7.2. Reimbursed accommodation

If your company's external consultant or contractor is not VAT registered, this can pose a problem for you, because they will pass on the VAT they pay in their overall fee, and you can't claim it back because you don't have a valid VAT invoice from them.

> EXAMPLE
>
> They incur a hotel bill of £1,000 plus VAT of £175 in connection with the work they are doing for you. Because they are not VAT registered they pass on the total cost to you, i.e. £1,175, and you have no VAT to reclaim on your next VAT return.

19.7.3. Other direct costs

If the self-employed person purchases tools or materials to use on a specific job for your business, can you recover the VAT on these? Yes, the VAT incurred is your input VAT providing: **(1)** in the case of tools, they become the property of your business; or **(2)** in the case of materials, they are incorporated into, and become a component cost of, the supply by your business to the final customer.

Maximising VAT recovery

19

19.7.4. Setting the terms and conditions

Conditions. If you meet some simple conditions, your business can recover the VAT. These are that: **(1)** they incur the expenditure only in respect of your business; **(2)** they receive no payment from the end customer; and **(3)** your business actually reimburses the individual who then hands over the VAT invoice.

TIP

If the contractor isn't VAT-registered, explain that you would like to treat any reimbursement of expenses as if they were your own expenses in order to maximise your VAT recovery.

TIP

Remember to obtain the invoice from the self-employed person for your company's records and process it in the same way as reimbursements made to employees, but not through the payroll - to avoid confusion about the freelancer's status.

TIP

If the expenses are substantial, offer to contract for and pay these direct in the contract with the freelancer. This way the VAT is available to reclaim right from the start.

Note. It's always possible that if you are visited by the VATman he will query this treatment. If he does, quote his own internal guidance, which states that this is acceptable.

KEY POINTS

Maximising VAT claims
- if your company is registered for VAT, it can generally reclaim VAT on business expenses
- have strict guidelines in your expenses policy about VAT receipts.

No receipts at all
- a VAT return is a self-declaration system although you have to keep specific evidence to back it up. You can claim up to four years' worth of missing VAT this way.

The VAT risk
- if a VAT officer finds that you have been claiming VAT back when you shouldn't have, he will ask for it back plus interest and penalties. However, he will only go back four years.

Trips to the EU
- if you conduct business overseas, your company can claim VAT back on many of the expenses incurred during the trip
- where your company incurs expenses in another EU state, unless its registered for VAT in the country concerned, it can claim back the foreign VAT by using the new cross-border electronic refund system.

Freelancers' expenses
- your company can still claim back the VAT on freelancers' expenses if incurred specifically in respect of your business. If the costs are substantial, avoid doubt by paying for the costs direct.

SECTION 2

Further angles and ideas

Why a Section 2?

In Section 2 of this book we have set out the ground rules for legitimately putting expenses through your business. Here you will see how much more of your money you will be able to keep from the Taxman's grasp. Never forget that the Taxman only ever gives you his biased interpretation of what is allowed. Use the following chapters to review the claims you are already making, as well as to find new ones. You'll be able to pick up suggestions and valuable tips on how to implement them. However, safety comes first. We identify the high, medium and low-risk ready-to-use strategies for you, so your decision-making process is made much easier (and safer).

CHAPTER 20

Company tax deduction

20.1. CLAIMING IT'S PART OF YOUR REMUNERATION

The key question to ask about any expense is will it actually be tax deductible for your company. This is where your total remuneration package with the company becomes so useful, as set out below.

In order to manage the business, a company has to attract and retain key employees. The cost of this usually meets the wholly and exclusively test, provided it's not excessive for the duties performed. Therefore, if you reassess your remuneration package (as an employee) to include in it a particular expense you would like the company to incur (as a benefit-in-kind for yourself) this is, in our opinion, wholly and exclusively for the purposes of the trade.

Company law. Remember, directors' remuneration is determined by the shareholders at their General Meetings. If the shareholders can't decide what is necessary for the company's trade, who can, Mr Taxman?

However, if challenged on this "part of your remuneration" argument by the Taxman, you'll need to be able to provide him with a copy of what was agreed in writing between you and your company - both amongst the company board minutes and as an addition to your contract of employment.

EXAMPLE

Amendment to contract of employment:

"As from May 1 2011, the Company will contract and pay for the painting and decorating of two rooms in your principal private residence each year. This benefit-in-kind is from that date part of your remuneration package with the company and will be provided by it subject to the company having sufficient funds to do so."

Further, if you've gone to the trouble of getting you and your company's paperwork right, so that a company expense can be legitimately treated as a benefit-in-kind, make sure it also appears on your P11D. Otherwise the Taxman can start arguing that it's earnings and tax it more heavily.

20.2. NATIONAL MINIMUM WAGE

The remuneration defence against a wholly and exclusively attack relies on you actually having a contract of employment with your company. You might not have one at present because to do so automatically brings you within the National Minimum Wage (NMW) requirements and hence will incur a small tax bill.

EXAMPLE

In 2011/12 let's say you've planned to take £7,228 (52 x £139) (the tax and NI-free amount) by way of salary, from your company and the rest of what you need by way of dividends. This is less than the current NMW (currently at £5.93 per hour) for an adult working 40 hours a week for 52 weeks (including four weeks paid holiday) of the year, which for 2010/11 works out at £12,334. The income tax bill on this level of salary works out as:

TOTAL 2011/12 SALARY OF £12,334	TAX RATE	£
On first £7,228	0%	0.00
On balance of £5,106	20%	1,021.20
Total income tax bill		1,021.20
EEs' NI (£12,334 - £7,228)	12%	612.72
ERs' NI (on £12,334 - £7,072)	13.8%	726.16
Total NI cost		1,338.88
Total tax and NI		2,360.08
Less CT deduction (*)	20%	(1,166.43)
Net tax cost of extra salary		1,193.65

(*) On extra salary plus employers' NI (£5,106 + £726.16 = £5,832.16).

In our opinion, for a small additional tax cost (in our example £1,080) of complying with the NMW you can get thousands of pounds of personal expenses classed as tax deductible in the company, under the banner of it being an agreed and documented addition to your contract of employment.

20.3.   BOARD MINUTES

Some time in the future the Taxman may enquire into your company's expenses. If so, he likes to put his own spin on your innocent actions. But there is something you can do now with your company's board minutes that will later stop him in his tracks.

You make many decisions, any one of which could have tax implications. If you are investigated and the Taxman thinks he can collect more tax, he will say that the decision you made was for the "purpose of avoiding tax". But if you can show otherwise, the law is on your side, and this only takes a minute.

He may try, but the Taxman has no right to tell you how to run your business. He can apply tax law but he will have trouble making it stick in borderline areas if you can show how the expenditure was intended to benefit the business.

Rule of thumb. Generally, any note of, for example, a telephone call or a meeting, made at the time or shortly afterwards can be produced in court as evidence in a dispute. A note made at the time shows what you were thinking - your intentions were good.

The directors of a company may have to consult each other, albeit informally. But some of these meetings have to be on a formal basis so that decisions taken are recorded as board minutes - which then form a statutory record. Boring, but necessary for company law purposes.

Most company minute books are on a shelf somewhere gathering dust. All they usually contain are a few pages of annual meetings, share allotments and directors' appointments. But they can be used to record other matters such as the leasing or purchase of premises and agreement to loans and/or bank overdrafts. In practice these things are considered before the meeting and are only put to the board for approval. So all that gets recorded is the decision. But this can be used to stay one step ahead of the Taxman.

EXAMPLE

A board minute could include a commercial reason for the company agreeing to add decorating arrangements to your remuneration package with the company. It might read as follows: *"In recognition of your contribution to the company and to avoid you spending time away from company business at key times to undertake DIY, the company has decided that as part of your remuneration package it will contract and pay for the painting and decorating of two rooms in your principal private residence each year. This is, of course, subject to the company having sufficient funds to do so."*

TIP

You can spike the Taxman's guns by recording your good intentions in a board minute at the time you make your decision. In cases where you think there may be a problem, post the signed minutes to the board members' home addresses. Keep yours and the envelope it came in to prove it was done at the time.

To charge penalties, the Taxman needs to show you were careless in your tax affairs. A timely minute can make that charge of negligence difficult to sustain.

For the avoidance of doubt, record your intentions in a board minute now. If, down the line, the Taxman wants to put another spin on things, you've put up a stop sign. This way you stay one step ahead of him.

KEY POINTS

- use the following chapters to review the claims you are already making as well as to find new ones
- reassess your remuneration package to include in it a particular expense you would like the company to incur
- you might need a contract of employment with your company. To do so brings you within the National Minimum Wage (NMW) requirements
- any note of a meeting made at the time or shortly afterwards can be produced as evidence in a dispute.

CHAPTER 21

Use of home by a company

21.1. THE EXPENSE

Taking things home to work on or even making that important conference call at home needs somewhere you can shut yourself away from the rest of the household. When it's company business could the company pay you a flat rate for this "use of home as office"?

The standard tax treatment for any such payment would be for the company to claim a deduction for it, but then to put it on your annual return of benefits and expenses (P11D). Like all entries from the P11D, this has to go on the employment page of your self-assessment tax return as income for you. But then you put down the same figure on the next page as an "expense incurred in doing your job" - hence claiming a tax deduction. Income (P11D) now matches expenditure (claim) giving zero tax bills. However, your claim for expenses incurred when working at home might not be worth the ink used as it's almost impossible in practice to get it past the Taxman as being "necessary".

£3 a week for additional costs

Instead, where there is a formalised agreement to work at home, the first £3 a week of any payment will be tax and NI-free in all cases. Higher payments may also be tax-free where evidence can be provided by you of the additional expense incurred in carrying out your duties from home.

Note. There is no wholly, exclusive and necessary condition here.

Renting alternative

A more lucrative alternative would be to get the payment from your company treated as rent instead of expenses. The company will get a tax deduction for the rent paid (provided it's not excessive) and if the rental income equals your own costs you will have a zero tax bill again.

What you're then left with is simply deciding what expenses are properly attributable to the provision of (furnished) accommodation to your company. The total of these is then used to set the level of rent received from the company. You can charge your company as little rent as you wish for using your property; it does not have to be at market value but it must not exceed it.

Expenses would include an appropriate proportion of heating and lighting costs, maintenance and repair costs and a proportion of mortgage interest, plus any expenses you incur at your company's specific request.

Back up this rental income assertion with a formal rent or licence agreement between you and the company and the property owners, i.e. you (and your spouse if owned jointly). This doesn't need to be a complicated document but does need to specify what has been agreed.

Broadband

In many businesses there is a clear need for directors and other employees to create, submit or receive and comment on work whilst at home. For example, the last minute agenda for the board meeting together with all the documents that are going to be discussed. However, there are tax consequences of the company paying for a broadband Internet connection to facilitate this.

Your company could pay a cash allowance towards your Internet costs related to work. You then claim a tax deduction on your tax return for the actual cost of business calls. The problem is that both income tax and NI (employees' and employers') is payable on the rental plus private calls.

The alternative is to have any bill (from the service provider) in the name of the employer, not you. The advantage of this is that your company doesn't have to put it through your payroll as it's classed as a benefit-in-kind.

Once again there is a tax cost. You're taxable on the monthly connection charge (including VAT). Yes, there's no employees' NI, but your company has to pay employers' NI on this benefit-in-kind. It is significantly cheaper than you paying out for broadband personally; however, you do have to pay some income tax. Unfortunately, some broadband providers will not allow a company-billed connection at a domestic address, so you would need to go down the route of reclaiming the expense from the company.

Your company will get a tax deduction for the rent paid (provided it's not excessive). And if the rental income is matched by your expenses, you will have a zero tax bill. You avoid arguing with the Taxman whether these expenses are wholly, exclusively and necessarily for the furtherance of your job. If sold, you would not pay any Capital Gains Tax on the home office part of your house, if it were a common area. So use it for private as well as business purposes.

Non-domestic use

Could business rates be due on this non-domestic use of part of your home? The current consensus is that provided you are not being visited by clients, then this is not a problem. However, in order to prevent the loss of principal private residence relief on this part of your home when you sell it, use it for private as well as business purposes, e.g. keep the exercise bike or guest bed in the room.

21.2.   WHAT ARE THE POTENTIAL TAX SAVINGS?

Paying £3 a week for additional costs means another £104 tax and NI-free a year that your company can pay you.

If the company pays you, for example, an additional flat rate of £50 a week (£2,600 p.a.) for use of home as office, but the Taxman wants to treat this as additional net salary, you could end up paying additional income tax and employees' NI of £1,883 (£2,600/58 x 42), as a higher rate taxpayer, plus employers' NI on this for 2011/12 would be a further £619.

If you can get the £50 treated as rent but matched with £50 worth of expenses, there will be no tax or NI to pay.

21.3.   THE PAPERWORK

By taking the following steps you will be making sure that there is no room for a challenge by the Taxman. And with all the paperwork done correctly there should be no risk of penalties arising at a later date either.

21.3.1.   The board minute

Remember, any expense charged in the company's accounts has to meet the "wholly and exclusively" test that we talked about earlier. Getting a formal board minute drawn up demonstrates to the Taxman that the benefit was agreed by the company as a way of rewarding you for your services.

There is no need for any special wording, just a statement of the facts as a record for future reference.

EXAMPLE

"Meeting of the Board of Directors of XYZ Limited on .... at ....

It was resolved that the company will pay rent to .... for office facilities (including a broadband connection) at .... (insert address). The rate to be reviewed annually under the terms and conditions of a formal licence agreement.

Signed .... company secretary."

21.3.2.   Rental agreement

Back up this payment for office facilities with a licence agreement between you and your company setting out formal terms and conditions.

21.3.3.   On the VAT return

There's no VAT involved in this expense.

21.3.4. On your P11D

No entry required.

21.3.5. In the company's accounts

Although there are no special disclosure requirements, if you include the payment for rent under "rent and rates" it reinforces your position that it's a business expense.

21.3.6. On your tax return

You'll need to record the rent you receive from your company as rental income on your tax return. Remember to claim the costs of supplying this facility to your company (in line with any specific requirements it might have, e.g. the cost of 20MB broadband access).

21.4.   LOW, MEDIUM AND HIGH-RISK STRATEGIES

21.4.1. Low-risk

Getting the paperwork right as described above cuts all risk down to an absolute minimum.

21.4.2. Medium-risk

If it's unclear that the payment is rent, there's a risk that it will be treated as net salary and the Taxman will come looking for tax and NI on the gross equivalent.

21.4.3. High-risk

You pay yourself a round sum allowance from the company for the use of your home as an office. If discovered, the Taxman will want to treat this as net salary that needs grossing-up for unpaid tax and NI, plus interest and penalties to boot.

CHAPTER 22

Garden maintenance

22.1. THE EXPENSE

You've heard from a colleague that they get their gardening paid for by the company. The Taxman is particular about private expenditure but you know there must be grey areas. Is this one?

If your company pays for any private expenditure of a director or employee, this will generally be taxed as a benefit-in-kind and the company will pay Class 1A NI on it at 13.8%. At worst, the Taxman will ask for the additional tax and NI on additional earnings from the company. So when your friend says their company is paying for their own gardening tax-free this is not the full story.

However, how would the Taxman find out that your friend was doing this anyway? For starters, the company has a duty to put such expenditure on an annual benefits declaration. If it doesn't and it's found out, say, during a visit from the Taxman, there will be overdue tax, interest and penalties to pay. Although not totally tax-free, there are still tax savings to be had by having you gardening expenses paid for by your company but treated as a benefit-in-kind.

There is, however, a definite grey area when it comes to indoor gardening.

Office plants

Let's say your company buys some plants from a garden centre to improve the working environment in your office. Is this tax deductible? We think so on the basis that this is an acceptable cost of running a modern-day office. The company will also need things like watering cans, watering trays, plant food, sprays, support sticks etc. to help these plants survive the rigours of office life. For those that don't survive, your company will have to buy replacements.

What's to say that some of these potted plants and related items don't end up in your home rather than the office? Or you took them home for emergency recovery treatment and never got around to bringing them back; is this a potential tax problem? The amounts involved are likely to relatively small (a trivial benefit) and so not picked up by either you or the Taxman.

22.2. WHAT IT MIGHT COST

If you go down the route of including gardening maintenance as part of your remuneration package, what will this cost you in tax?

Tony has been too busy to look after his garden. It needs a good blitz to get it into shape. After that it should be easy to maintain. Let's say the blitz will cost him £1,000 - including some tree surgery. But ongoing maintenance is only likely to be £50 per month. He thinks the company's own maintenance contractors do a good job so he asks them if they'll arrange the work for him. Where does he stand for tax if the company pays for the lot?

If classed as a benefit-in-kind, Tony (as a higher-rate taxpayer) might pay income tax of £520 (£1,300 @40%) on the £1,000 blitz plus £300 for six months' ongoing work. The company would also have to pay employers' NI on this benefit of £179 (£1,300 @13.8%). Total tax bill £699 (£520 + £179).

22.3.   WHAT ARE THE POTENTIAL TAX SAVINGS?

If you pay for gardening/indoor plants out of your own pocket, then it's likely to come from income that has already suffered tax. If it's income from your company, this money has probably been extracted as either salary or dividends. If you can reduce your tax bill by getting the company to pay direct then you are in a winning situation. So what are the potential tax savings?

22.3.1.   Not treated as additional salary

If, instead of being taxed as a benefit-in-kind, the gardening outlay is classed as additional salary for you, the tax bill goes through the roof. The Taxman will say that to have £1,300 to spend you should have paid tax and NI on a gross addition to your salary from the company. As a 40% taxpayer that's £2,241 gross pay (£1,300/58 x 100), so he'll come looking for £941 in income tax and employees' NI plus £309 at 13.8% employers' NI. Total tax bill £1,250. Going down the benefit-in-kind route saves tax of about £550 (£1,250 - £699).

Although the company pays employers' NI on the cost to it of the service, this is less than the NI it would pay on the equivalent salary.

22.3.2.   Corporation Tax

Your company will get a tax deduction for the expenditure itself and the employers' NI on the benefit-in-kind. You would not get a tax deduction for it. This leaves more money in the company for you to take out at a later stage. **Rule of thumb.** The company will save Corporation Tax on this benefit-in-kind (net of VAT) at the rate of 20%. You will save employees' NI at the rate of either 12% or 2%.

22.4. THE PAPERWORK

You've reassessed your remuneration package to include maintaining your garden as a benefit-in-kind for yourself. What your company therefore needs to do is put this arrangement in writing - both in the company board minutes and as an addition to your contract of employment.

After the end of the tax year, your company then has to get its external reporting right to the Taxman by including this benefit-in-kind on your P11D.

22.4.1. The board minute

Use a board minute to acknowledge this change to your remuneration package.

EXAMPLE

The board minute covering Jim's "ground force" option reads as follows: *"In recognition of your contribution to the company and to avoid you spending time away from company business at key times to undertake gardening duties the company has decided that as part of your remuneration package it will contract and pay for the cost of a maintenance blitz/monthly maintenance for the garden in your principal private residence, up to a value of £1,000 p.a. This is, of course, subject to the company having sufficient funds to do so."*

You're not trying to hide anything from the Taxman; in fact you want this out in the open and agreed.

TIP

Write to your advisor telling them what you're doing so that it can be included on your P11D. This also helps them to assess your tax position.

22.4.2. Your contract of employment

Your company needs to put this addition to your remuneration package in writing as an amendment to your contract of employment.

EXAMPLE

Amendment to contract of employment.

"As from November 30 2008, the company will contract and pay for gardening at your principal private residence up to a specified value to be agreed annually with the company. Anything in excess of this you will reimburse the company for. This benefit-in-kind is from this date part of your remuneration package with the company and will be provided by it subject to the company having sufficient funds to do so."

22.4.3. Contract with/invoice from the supplier

You need the cost of gardening to be treated as a benefit-in-kind. Therefore, the contract with the gardener must be negotiated by, addressed to and clearly seen to be a liability of the company (not yours).

22.4.4. On the VAT return

> **TIP**
>
> If the company has claimed VAT on the gardening costs, pay a nominal sum to it for the ongoing service, say, £10 per month. You don't have to pay this contribution monthly; just one sum before the end of the tax year will do the trick. Treat this as inclusive of VAT and include the output VAT on your company's VAT return. (On £10 that's output VAT of £1.67 (£10 x 20/120) Otherwise, the VATman can disallow the company's claim for input VAT on the whole invoice.

Any contribution you make towards the company's cost reduces the potential tax charge both for you and the company.

22.4.5. On your P11D

Your company needs to enter the VAT-inclusive cost(s) (even if it has already claimed the VAT) of maintaining your garden on your P11D.

22.4.6. In the company's accounts

Transfer the cost of this work out of, say, maintenance and into staff costs. This reinforces your company's argument that it's part of your remuneration package and hence it can claim a tax deduction for this expense.

22.4.7. Your tax return

You simply take the figure given to you by the company for your P11D benefit and put it on your tax return. No further disclosures are required by you.

22.5. LOW, MEDIUM AND HIGH-RISK STRATEGIES

22.5.1. Low-risk

If you get the paperwork right, the low-risk strategy is the benefit-in-kind route outlined above.

22.5.2. Medium-risk

The company does not get a tax deduction for the costs of maintaining your garden for you because the Taxman doesn't accept that this expense is "wholly and exclusively" for the purpose of the company's trade. This would be the case if it wasn't clear that this was part of your remuneration package.

22.5.3. High-risk

Your company contracts and pays for "maintenance" work. The invoice is made out for one amount that includes work at all locations (including at your home). Since there is only one invoice to cover the maintenance contract it's going to be difficult for anyone to pick out any private expenditure. You wait six years and hope the Taxman doesn't pick this up before then. If he does, there will be the overdue tax, interest and penalties to pay.

CHAPTER 23

Gifts

23.1. THE EXPENSE

Buying gifts for your partner and putting them through the company is obviously a red rag to a bull as far as the Taxman is concerned. He will want his share of tax and NI on what he sees as your remuneration. If he finds out, that is.

The more creative amongst you might do this anyway and then describe the expenses on a petty cash voucher. For example; *"£150 digital radio for the staff restroom"* or *"£30 plants for the office"* thus misdirecting any potential challenge to your expenses from your accountant or the Taxman. Whilst we cannot condone this, we, like the Taxman, know it goes on. But why go to all that trouble when there are legitimate ways to get the company to pay for it, particularly if your partner works for the company.

A romantic dinner for two

Any expense for the benefit of staff is normally deductible against the company's profits but taxable on the employee. But there's a concession which could make a meal completely tax-free. Each tax year (April 6 to April 5) the company can spend up to £150 per head on staff events, without any taxable benefit assessed on the employee.

> **TIP**
>
> If your partner is your only employee and you haven't already spent the whole £150 per employee on another event, such as attending a summer concert, then why not have a Christmas party? As long as the total bill for this year's staff events comes to less than £150 per employee, it'll be tax and NI-free for both of you. Try and formalise the outing as a works do by recording the booking in the company minutes. And make sure the company pays directly for the meal otherwise it's an expense to be repaid to you as a director, which may not be allowable.

A diamond ring?

If your partner is also a director or earns at least £8,500 a year from the company (including benefits), then getting the company to buy them, say, a diamond ring, as a reward for services could still work out cheaper than paying for it yourself.

Box of chocolates etc.

Although there's technically no monetary limit below which gifts to staff are considered tax-free, the Taxman recognises that some gifts (not money or vouchers) should be ignored as they are so "trivial" in nature that it would cost too much to collect. The examples given in the Taxman's manual include a bottle of wine or a box of chocolates. But the gift must not be seen as a reward for services or it will be taxable.

TIP

If your partner works for the company, the gift of a box of chocolates can legitimately be put through the company. Just make sure it's recorded as a goodwill gift.

What's considered a small gift? A turkey or a box of chocolates can cost anything from a couple of pounds to over £30, and a bottle of wine could cost several hundred pounds. Small to one company could be very expensive to another. Do other gifts count? The Taxman has only cited turkeys, chocolates and wine as examples. These would be no use to a teetotal vegetarian on a diet.

TIP

Before you (and your employees) receive any trivial benefits, write to your tax office seeking confirmation and agreement that you can leave the benefits you wish to provide off your P11D reporting.

23.2.   WHAT ARE THE POTENTIAL TAX SAVINGS?

If you pay for gifts out of your own pocket, then it's likely that this comes out of income that's already suffered tax. If it's income from your company, this money has probably been extracted as either salary or dividends. If you can reduce your tax bill by getting the company to pay direct then you are in a winning situation. So what are the potential tax savings?

EXAMPLE 1

To have £300 in your pocket to pay for a nice evening out, it will cost you £75 in income tax (as a higher-rate taxpayer) to take this out of your company as a dividend. Total cost of meal to you: £375. However, if your company pays for a staff event it can claim back any VAT it's been charged and get a tax deduction for all the costs associated with the event. On a £300 bill that's potentially £50 (£300 x 20/120) of recoverable VAT for your company and reduction in its Corporation Tax bill of £50 (£300 - £50 = £250 x 20%). Net cost of the event to the company £200. Total saving £175 (£375 - £200).

If you pay for a diamond ring for your partner out of dividends, then, as a higher-rate taxpayer, you'll have to pay tax on those dividends. If you take £1,000 out as dividends, your extra tax bill will be £250. However, if the company pays directly for the ring, it can be included on your partner's P11D, they might only pay 20% tax on the benefit (£200) and the company will pay 13.8% employers' NI (£138). However, as long as you can prove the gift is for business purposes (record it in the company minutes as a reward for services), the company will get 20% tax relief for the gift plus employers' NI (20% of £1,138 = £228) so the overall tax paid is £110. A saving of £140.

23.3. THE PAPERWORK

Your company has to get its internal and external reporting right.

23.3.1. The board minute

In a board minute include a commercial reason for the company agreeing to include specific gifts as part of the remuneration package.

EXAMPLE

The board minute reads as follows: *"In recognition of your contribution, the company has decided that as part of your remuneration package, it will contract and pay for an item of personal jewellery, up to a value of £1,000. This is, of course, subject to the company having sufficient funds to do so."*

You're not trying to hide anything from the Taxman; in fact, you want this out in the open and agreed.

TIP

Write to your advisor telling them what you're doing so that it can be included on your P11D.

23.3.2. Your contract of employment

Your company needs to put any addition to your remuneration package in writing as an amendment to your contract of employment.

EXAMPLE

Amendment to contract of employment:

"As from November 30 2011, the company will contract and pay for an item of personal jewellery, up to a value of £1,000. This is, of course, subject to the company having sufficient funds to do so."

23.3.3. Contract with/invoice from the supplier

You need the jewellery to be treated as a benefit-in-kind. As such, the contract with the jeweller needs to be negotiated by, addressed to, and be clearly a liability of the company (not yours).

23.3.4. On the VAT return

Staff events

If a guest comes to an event, ask them to pay a nominal contribution towards costs, say, £10. Treat this as inclusive of VAT and include the output VAT on your company's VAT return. (On £10 that's output VAT of £1.67 (£10 x 20/120). Otherwise, the VATman can disallow the company's claim for input VAT on the guest's share of the costs.

You can also legitimately give staff gifts, up to the value of £50 plus VAT in any twelve-month period, and claim back any VAT you were charged in buying them.

23.3.5. On your P11D

Your company needs to enter the VAT-inclusive cost(s) (even if the company has already claimed the VAT) of the gift on your P11D.

23.3.6. In the company's accounts

Transfer the cost of this gift out of general expenses (if that's where it's ended up) and into staff costs. This reinforces your company's argument that it is part of your remuneration package and hence it can claim a tax deduction for it.

23.3.7. Your tax return

You simply take whatever the figure given to you by the company for your P11D benefits and put them on your tax return. No further disclosures are required by you.

23.4. LOW, MEDIUM AND HIGH-RISK STRATEGIES

23.4.1. Low-risk

Putting gifts for yourself through your company's expenses is risky. However, treating your spouse (as a member of staff) to a meal can legitimately be claimed if it's part of a staff event.

A potential tax liability exists with even minor gifts. However, it seems the Taxman will not bother to collect it. Write to your tax office asking permission to leave specific trivial benefits off your company's P11Ds.

23.4.2. Medium-risk

The company doesn't get a tax deduction for the costs of gifts to staff because the Taxman doesn't accept that this expense is "wholly and exclusively" for the purpose of the company's trade. This would be the case if it wasn't clear that this was a staff event or a goodwill gesture to staff or that it's part of your remuneration package.

23.4.3. High-risk

Describe the presents on a petty cash voucher. For example, *"£150 digital radio for the staff restroom"* (actually at home) or *"£30 plants for the office"* (they were for your partner) thus misdirecting any potential challenge to your expenses from your accountant or the Taxman. You then wait six years and hope the Taxman doesn't pick this up before then. If he does, there will be the overdue tax, interest and penalties to pay.

CHAPTER 24

Language lessons

24.1. THE EXPENSE

Your company can get a full tax deduction for any work-related training it provides to its employees, which includes you as a director. "Work-related" means any skill you may have need of at work either now or in the future (or even when you work in a voluntary capacity on behalf of the firm, such as helping a local charity).

For example, as almost any company with a website can expect to receive product enquiries from other countries, so foreign language skills are necessary for all staff, particularly those who may need to negotiate overseas contracts.

The range of courses the company can pay for is quite extensive. For example, if your staff have to drive as part of their job you can provide advanced driving lessons, or for trainees who don't yet hold a driving licence you can pay for a full driving course including the test fees.

24.2. WHAT IT MIGHT COST

You can expect to pay about £50 per week for two hours' instruction from a qualified teacher, for at least ten weeks, to achieve fluency. Interestingly, there won't be any tax cost associated with this being paid for by your company if it's work-related.

24.3. WHAT ARE THE POTENTIAL TAX SAVINGS?

EXAMPLE

Let's say you pay about £50 per week for two hours' instruction from a qualified teacher, for at least ten weeks. That's £500 from your after-tax income, which to put you in funds to do so will cost your company £981 in gross wages and NI (£500/58% = £862 gross wages + £119 employers' NI), or £785 after Corporation Tax (CT) relief at 20%.

If your company contracts directly with your language teacher to provide your personal lessons, the cost to it will be £500, but that expense will be fully tax deductible as staff training. So the net cost to a company paying 20% CT is £400 (80% x £500). That's a 49% saving for your company ((£785 - £400) / £785) compared with paying you extra salary.

24.4. THE PAPERWORK

Trap. If the employee picks up the cost of the course and you reimburse those fees, the amount paid will be taxed as a benefit-in-kind.

24.4.1. The board minute

In your board minute include a commercial reason for the company agreeing to courses for employees (including directors).

EXAMPLE

The board minute agreeing to "work-related" training might reads as follows:

"The company has decided to provide work-related training for its employees, which includes directors. "Work-related" means any skill the employee may have need of at work either now or in the future, or even when the employee works in a voluntary capacity on behalf of the firm. In particular, via our website we expect to receive product enquiries from other countries, so foreign language skills are necessary for all staff, particularly those, such as the directors, who may need to negotiate overseas contracts. This is, of course, subject to the company having sufficient funds to do so."

You're not trying to hide anything from the Taxman; in fact you want this out in the open and agreed.

TIP

Write to your advisor telling them what you're doing so that it can be excluded from your P11D, under the exemption for work-related training.

24.4.2. Your contract of employment

Your company needs to put the availability of work-related training in writing as an amendment to your contract of employment.

EXAMPLE

Amendment to contract of employment:

"As from November 30 2011, the company will, from time to time, contract and pay for work-related training. This will be provided by it subject to the company having sufficient funds to do so."

24.4.3. Contract with/invoice from the supplier

You need the work-related training course to be a contractual liability of the company, not your own. As such, the contract with the course provider needs to be negotiated by, addressed to and clearly be seen as a liability of the company (not yours).

24.4.4. On the VAT return

Any VAT charged by the course provider can be claimed back by your company on its VAT return.

24.4.5. On your P11D

No entry required.

24.4.6. In the company's accounts

Book the course costs under something like "training" or "staff costs".

24.4.7. Your tax return

No entry required.

24.5. LOW, MEDIUM AND HIGH-RISK STRATEGIES

24.5.1. Low-risk

If you get the paperwork right the low-risk strategy is the one outlined above.

24.5.2. Medium-risk

The company doesn't get a tax deduction for the costs of such training because the Taxman doesn't accept that this expense does not meet the conditions of the exemption. This would be the case if the course wasn't for a skill needed at work.

24.5.3. High-risk

You book a course of flying or scuba diving lessons in your own name, but have the company pay for them. Booked as staff training in your accounts no entries are made on your P11D in the relevant tax year. You now wa\\it six years and hope the Taxman doesn't pick this up before then. If he does, there will be the overdue tax, interest and penalties to pay.

CHAPTER 25

Magazine subscriptions

25.1. THE EXPENSE

The Taxman publishes a list of those subscriptions which he considers you can get a tax deduction for. This can be found at http://www.hmrc.gov.uk/list3/list3.pdf. But what this doesn't tell you is whether the subscription to your favourite magazine is tax deductible.

Subscriptions to magazines, newspapers etc. will be deductible if they are "wholly and exclusively" for the purpose of the trade. Classic examples of this are subscriptions to business-to-business publications like monthly trade magazines. But what about your newspapers/favourite magazines (Top Gear, Hello etc.) you get at home? Not really tax deductible unless…

You probably have a reception area in the office for visitors, or a staff restroom where it would be logical to have a pile of magazines to read and keep up-to-date.

TIP

Get the company to pay direct for your favourite magazines or reimburse you for them. These can either be delivered to the office or you bring them in from home. Either way they end up in reception or the restroom. That's what the company bought them for wasn't it?

And another thing. With that many magazines what are you going to keep them in? How about a nice antique oak magazine/newspaper rack? Paid for by the company of course but very similar to the one you've got at home. Your company, your taste.

25.2. WHAT IT MIGHT COST

How much is an annual subscription? Your company could probably get a "twelve issues for the price of ten, plus a free gift" offer, as a new subscriber to a publication. So if each magazine had an issue price of £4.50, the cost to your company would be £45 for an annual subscription.

25.3. WHAT ARE THE POTENTIAL TAX SAVINGS?

If you pay for the magazine subscription out of your own pocket, then it's likely to be from income that's already suffered tax. If it's income from your company, this money has probably been extracted as either salary or dividends. If you can reduce your tax bill by getting the company to pay direct then you are in a winning situation. So what are the potential tax savings?

Some car magazines can cost £4.50 a month, that's £54 a year. Four of these gets you to over £200 a year. If you pay out, say, as a 40% taxpayer, that's spending gross salary of about £345 (£200/58%). If the company pays for it but puts it down as a benefit-in-kind, you could end up paying tax of £80 (£200 x 40%). So let the company pay for it and include it under staff welfare costs - along with the tea, coffee etc. It's just another office expense. There's no tax bill for you this way.

25.4. THE PAPERWORK

25.4.1. Contract with/invoice from the supplier

You need the publication to be treated as "wholly and exclusively" for the business. As such, the subscription with the publisher/newsagent needs to be addressed to and clearly be a liability of the company (not yours).

25.4.2. On your P11D

No entry required.

25.4.3. In the company's accounts

Include magazines under, say, staff welfare costs - along with the tea, coffee etc. It's just another office expense.

25.4.4. Your tax return

No entry required.

25.5. LOW, MEDIUM AND HIGH-RISK STRATEGIES

25.5.1. Low-risk

Your company buys magazines for the office, which you read second-hand.

25.5.2. Medium-risk

The company does not get a tax deduction for the costs of magazine subscriptions because the Taxman doesn't accept that this expense is "wholly and exclusively" for the purpose of the company's trade. This would be the case if it wasn't clear that this was part of a normal business activity.

25.5.3. High-risk

If your favourite magazine ends up at the office, who's to say it's not part of general office costs. So get the company to pay for the subscription to the magazine, you just act as postman.

CHAPTER 26

Paying for a holiday

26.1. THE EXPENSE

You need a holiday. Having decided you are definitely going you might well ask yourself the question, why is it that my company can't just pay for this well-earned break?

It's perfectly legal for the company to pay for a director's or employee's holiday and get a tax deduction for it against the company's profits for Corporation Tax (CT) purposes, as long as the payment gets taxed as part of their remuneration package.

26.2. WHAT IT MIGHT COST

EXAMPLE

Let's take a £3,000 family holiday to be either funded out of net bonus, paid direct by your company or covered by a special dividend.

	BONUS(£)	BENEFIT (£)	DIVIDEND (£)
Holiday cost (net)	3,000	3,000	3,000
Income tax and EEs' NI	2,172	1,200	750
ERs' NI @ 13.8%	714	414	-
Total cost	5,886	4,614	3,750
CT saving (*)	(1,177)	(683)	-
Net cost	4,709	3,931	3,750

(*) CT saving on : Bonus cost of £5,886 @20% = 1,177

Benefit-in-kind cost of £3,414 @20% = £683

If the company paid you an additional bonus to cover the cost of a holiday it should get a CT deduction for this (plus the associated employers' NI cost). But this can work out a bit expensive. A £3,000 holiday would require a gross bonus before taxes of say £5,172 (£3,000/58%) and result in an employers' NI bill of £714 (£5,172 x 13.8%). The company spends £5,886.

26.3. WHAT ARE THE POTENTIAL TAX SAVINGS?

If you pay for the holiday out of your own pocket, then it's likely that this comes out of income that has already suffered tax. If it's income from your company, this money has probably been extracted as either salary or dividends. If you can reduce your tax bill by getting the company to pay direct then you are in a winning situation. So what are the potential tax savings?

A trip invoiced to and paid for in the company's name is potentially a benefit-in-kind, i.e. it's not capable of conversion into cash by you. A £3,000 holiday would cost you £1,200 (£3,000 x 40%) in additional income tax and your company NI on the benefit-in-kind, i.e. 13.8% of £3,000 = £414. The company spends £3,414 and the Taxman collects £1,200 from you. The CT saving is £4,683 (£3,414 x 20%).

A dividend of £3,000 would save on NI compared to a benefit-in-kind but is not tax deductible for your company, so no CT saving.

26.4. THE PAPERWORK

You've reassessed your remuneration package to include in it a holiday expense you would like the company to incur as a benefit-in-kind for yourself. What your company needs to do is put this arrangement in writing - both amongst the company board minutes and as an addition to your contract of employment.

Once the holiday has been completed, your company then has to get its external reporting right, first to the VATman, then in its accounts and finally to the Taxman on its P11D.

26.4.1. The board minute

In your board minute include a commercial reason for the company agreeing to include holiday arrangements as part of your remuneration package.

EXAMPLE

The board minute covering the holiday could read as follows:

"In recognition of your contribution to the company and the need to take a break to renew your enthusiasm and freshness for your day-to-day tasks, the company has decided that as part of your remuneration package, it will contract and pay for one two-week holiday each year.

However, this must be taken during the company's deemed quiet period which is currently the month of August. This is, of course, subject to the company having sufficient funds to do so."

You're not trying to hide anything from the Taxman; in fact you want this out in the open and agreed.

TIP

Write to your tax advisor telling them what you're doing so that it can be included on your P11D.

26.4.2. Your contract of employment

Your company needs to put this addition to your remuneration package in writing as an amendment to your contract of employment.

EXAMPLE

Amendment to contract of employment

"As from November 30 2011, the company will contract and pay for a two-week holiday each year. However, this must be taken during the company's deemed quiet period, which is currently the month of August. This benefit-in-kind is from that date part of your remuneration package with the company and will be provided by it subject to the company having sufficient funds to do so."

26.4.3. Contract with/invoice from the supplier

You need the holiday to be treated as a benefit-in-kind. As such the contract with the travel agent needs to be negotiated by, addressed to and clearly be seen as the liability of the company.

26.4.4. On the VAT return

Don't bother to claim the VAT back on the holiday.

26.4.5. On your P11D

Your company needs to enter the cost of the holiday in that tax year on your P11D.

26.4.6. In the company's accounts

Transfer the cost of this holiday out of travel and subsistence expenses and into staff costs. This reinforces your company's argument that it's part of your remuneration package and hence it can claim a tax deduction for it.

26.4.7. Your tax return

You simply take the figure given to you by the company for your P11D benefit and put it on your tax return. No further disclosures are required by you.

26

26.5. LOW, MEDIUM AND HIGH-RISK STRATEGIES

26.5.1. Low-risk

If you get the paperwork right, the low-risk strategy is the one outlined above.

26.5.2. Medium-risk

The company does not get a tax deduction for the costs of the holiday because the Taxman doesn't accept that this expense is "wholly and exclusively" for the purpose of the company's trade. This would be the case if it wasn't clear that this was part of your remuneration package.

26.5.3. High-risk

It's easy enough to identify the payment for a package holiday, e.g. an entry on the company credit card statement for £3,000 for Happy Holidays Limited. However, if you book it yourself with separate payments for flights, car hire and hotel accommodation you end up with different invoices/payments at different times to different companies. That's not so easy to trace.

When, say, the company credit card statement is analysed these company expenses could end up in travel (flights), motor expenses (car hire) and accommodation (hotel). All could be forgotten by the time it comes to preparing the company accounts, say, twelve months later. If these individual amounts don't stick out from the crowd within those expense headings, who's going to spot them?

It's an option but a risky one, of course, because of interest and penalties for not accounting to the Taxman for tax on either the additional salary to cover the holiday payments or the benefit-in-kind.

You could transfer the costs to your director's loan account to avoid penalties etc., but this would only be a temporary solution.

CHAPTER 27

Private tutors

27.1. THE EXPENSE

Saturday morning ballet or karate lessons were probably not what the government had in mind when it gave tax relief for childcare paid for by employers. But the Taxman has confirmed that as long as the teacher is an approved childcarer, any different activities (such as personal tuition) offered in the course of providing the childcare, will still be covered by the tax exemption. So how is this possible?

All employers can give their employees childcare vouchers, or pay for childcare directly worth up to £55 per week, with no tax or NI charges. This tax-free limit is per employee not per child, so if you have more than one child, or your spouse doesn't work, you lose out. This can be used for your child's education as well as care, as long as certain conditions are met.

Condition 1

The childcare vouchers, or direct payment by the company must be used for qualifying care provided before September 1 following the child's 15th birthday. This is generally the beginning of the school year eleven/end of year ten/the final year of compulsory schooling. So you can't use this tax break to pay for last minute GCSE or A-level exam tuition.

Qualifying care can be any form of care or supervised activity that is not part of the child's compulsory education. So as long as the subject of your child's extra lessons is not covered in compulsory school hours, it can be paid for directly by your company or with childcare vouchers up to the tax-free limit.

Condition 2

The care must be provided by a registered or approved childcarer. Unfortunately, most registered childminders are not also qualified to teach music, karate, Latin or whatever extra skill you want your child to learn.

However, specialist private teachers can register with the Department for Children, Schools and Families to become an approved childcarer if they provide their services in England (different regulations apply in Scotland and Wales). To do this the teacher must have: **(1)** a basic childcare qualification; **(2)** hold a first aid certificate appropriate to children and; **(3)** have a clean enhanced criminal records check. All of which you'd probably look for in a private tutor anyway.

If your company reimburses you for the tutor's fees, or pays a bill made out to you personally, the tax exemption doesn't apply.

TIP

Once a specialist private teacher has registered to become an approved childcarer, get your company to make arrangements

Private tutors

directly with them for the lessons to be provided to your child, and sign any contract required. The full cost of the lessons is then tax deductible for the company and the first £55 per week is tax and NI-free for you.

27.2. WHAT IT MIGHT COST

Because of the exemption for childcare vouchers there is no tax cost to you. Indeed, if you and your partner both work for the company that's a tax-free limit of £110 per week.

27.3. WHAT ARE THE POTENTIAL TAX SAVINGS?

If you pay for the tuition out of your own pocket, then it's likely that this comes out of income that has already suffered tax. If it's income from your company, this money has probably been extracted as either salary or dividends. If you can reduce your tax bill by getting the company to pay direct then you are in a winning situation.

Recent change. If you joined a childcare voucher (CV) scheme before April 6 2011, you can continue to receive tax and NI-free CVs as part of your salary package. The maximum tax saving for the employee is £572, £1,144 or £1,430 per year for basic rate, higher rate (40%) and additional rate (50%) taxpayers respectively. But those joining an employer's CV scheme after April 5 2011 will all get the same tax advantage of just £572. However, the NI advantage varies; those whose earnings are taxed at the basic rate can save up to £343 annually, but for those who pay tax at the higher or additional rate, it's only about £30.

Existing scheme members will be unaffected by the change, as long as they stay in their current employment and ensure any breaks in their voucher order last no longer than twelve months.

All employees who join the scheme after April 5 2011 will need to have their earnings estimated when they join the scheme and at the start of each tax year. Their eligible CV allowance will be recalculated at the start of each tax year.

If an employee's earnings change during the tax year, their CVs will only be affected from the start of the next tax year.

Employers will :

- need to establish a process for checking their scheme members' earnings when they join the scheme and at the start of each tax year
- need to keep a record of when each earnings check takes place

- continue to enjoy NI savings in respect of every scheme member. However, where employees' voucher orders are restricted by the new rules, employer NI savings will fall accordingly.

The bottom line is that CVs don't just offer tax and NI savings for employees. As an employer you can save NI by offering eligible staff CVs in place of an equal amount of salary, i.e. by using a salary sacrifice scheme.

TIP

This tax break isn't just for your staff; directors who incur childcare costs shouldn't overlook the opportunity to pay themselves up to £2,860 tax-free, with reduced NI, per year.

27.4. THE PAPERWORK

You've reassessed your remuneration package to include childcare vouchers, as a benefit-in-kind for yourself. What your company needs to do is put this arrangement in writing - as a new company policy, amongst the company board minutes and as an addition to your contract of employment.

27.5. THE CHILDCARE POLICY

Your company will need to have a written policy on childcare vouchers.

EXAMPLE

"The Company operates a childcare voucher scheme which is open to all employees. The scheme is implemented as a salary sacrifice arrangement where you exchange part of your salary for childcare vouchers.

The first £55 per week of the voucher's face value will be given to you tax and NI-free as long as the following conditions are met...... (same conditions as for the Taxman).

You will provide details of your childcare provider to the Company including their registration or approval number together with the date the relevant registration expires.

You must notify the Company of any changes in registration or approval status of your child's carer or changes in childcare arrangements.

The Company will provide you with a childcare voucher. You will then give this voucher to your qualifying childcare provider. The childcare provider will then sign the voucher and send it to the Company for reimbursement. There is no cost to the childcare provider in receiving payment through childcare vouchers."

27.5.1. Your contract of employment

Your company needs to put this addition to your remuneration package in writing as an amendment to your contract of employment.

EXAMPLE

Amendment to contract of employment:

"As from November 30 2011, you are entitled to opt for childcare vouchers as part of your remuneration package. This benefit-in-kind will be provided by the company subject to it having sufficient funds to do so."

27.5.2. On your P11D

No entry required within the tax and NI-free limit.

27.5.3. In the company's accounts

Record the cost of these childcare vouchers as "staff costs".

27.5.4. Your tax return

No entry required within the tax and NI-free limit.

27.6. LOW, MEDIUM AND HIGH-RISK STRATEGIES

27.6.1. Low-risk

If you get the paperwork right, the low-risk strategy is the one outlined above.

27.6.2. Medium-risk

The company does not get a tax deduction for the childcare vouchers because the Taxman doesn't accept that this expense is "wholly and exclusively" for the purpose of the company's trade. This would be the case if it wasn't clear that this was part of your remuneration package.

27.6.3. High-risk

Your company settles your account with a private tutor but records this as staff training. No entries are made on your P11D or tax return. You now wait six years and hope the Taxman doesn't pick this up before then. If he does, there will be the overdue tax, interest and penalties to pay.

CHAPTER 28

School fees

28.1. THE EXPENSE

With the cost of a private education running into thousands of pounds per term it would be nice if you could get the company to foot the bill. But if a company meets the personal liability of a director or other employee, then the Taxman will apply the "pecuniary liability principle" and there will be penalties added for not making the right declarations. But by following the rules set out below you can get your children's education paid for by the company without paying tax at penal rates.

28.2. WHAT ARE THE POTENTIAL TAX SAVINGS?

If you pay the tuition fees yourself, it will come from income that's already had tax deducted from it. However, if the company pays then you save some of the tax. The potential savings are examined below.

28.2.1. Savings on your salary

If the company pays for your child's education, the payments will be taxed under the benefit-in-kind rules on you as the director/employee.

The tax on this benefit will be less than what you would have normally paid under PAYE to get the same net amount of income to meet the school fees yourself. In addition, there won't be any employees' NI to pay either. The company will have an NI bill to pay, but once again it will be on a lesser amount than the salary equivalent.

28.2.2. Corporation Tax

Your company will be permitted to make a deduction in its accounts for the school fees, which means it pays less Corporation Tax. And because it's classed as a remuneration, the NI paid by the company on the benefit-in-kind gets tax relief too, leaving more money in the company for you to take out at a later date.

28.3. EXAMPLE

If the annual school fees were £15,000, this is the level of additional salary you would require after tax and NI has been deducted by the company. We can now compare the relative tax positions if the £15,000 is treated as net salary or as a benefit-in-kind.

28.3.1. You

	40% TAXPAYER (£)
Tax on salary £15,000 (x 42/58)	10,862
Tax on benefits of £15,000	6,000
Saving	4,862

28.3.2. Your company and employers' NI

	40% TAXPAYER (£)
Ers' NI on salary @ 13.8% of £25,862	3,569
Ers' on benefits @ 13.8% of £15,000	2,070
Saving	1,499

28.3.3. Corporation Tax saving on a benefit

	£
Corporation Tax on annual school fees (£15,000 @ 20%)	3,000
Corporation Tax on employers' NI (£2,070 @ 20%)	414
Saving	3,414

28.4. THE PAPERWORK

By taking the following steps you will make sure that there is no room for a challenge by the Taxman. And with all the paperwork in order there should be no risk of penalties arising at a later date either.

28.4.1. The board minute

Remember, any expense charged in the company's accounts has to meet the "wholly and exclusively" test. Getting a formal board minute drawn up demonstrates to the Taxman that the benefit was agreed on by the company as a way of rewarding you for your services to the company. There is no need for any special wording, just a statement of the facts as a record for future reference.

EXAMPLE

The following can be used as an example:

"Meeting of the Board of Directors of XYZ Limited on .... at ....

It was resolved that the company approve the payment of school fees of Mr X's children as part of his remuneration package.

This award has been made in recognition of his continuing contribution to the success of the company.

Signed .... company secretary."

28.4.2. Your contract of employment

Because this is a variation of your remuneration package you will need to incorporate it into your contract of employment by way of an addendum.

EXAMPLE

"As of .... the company will pay your children's school fees subject to the availability of funds. This benefit-in-kind is to be treated as part of your remuneration package with the company."

28.4.3. Contract with/invoice from the supplier

Warning. You need to get the school to make it absolutely clear that the liability for payment rests with the company and that they will not revert to you should there be any delay in settling the fees.

28.4.4. On the VAT return

Because there's no VAT chargeable on the provision of education there will be no VAT to reclaim on the school fees.

28.4.5. On your P11D

The value of the benefit-in-kind to be included in your P11D is the contracted value of the school fees in that tax year.

28.4.6. In the company's accounts

Although there are no special disclosure requirements, if you include the charge for the school fees within remuneration costs, this reinforces your position that it's part of your agreed package.

28.4.7. Your tax return

Simply transfer the values from your P11D to the relevant boxes on your tax return's employment pages. Any tax due will then be collected in the normal way.

28.5. LOW, MEDIUM AND HIGH-RISK STRATEGIES

28.5.1. Low-risk

If you get the paperwork right, the low-risk strategy is the one outlined above.

28.5.2. Medium-risk

The company does not get a tax deduction for the costs of school fees because the Taxman doesn't accept that this expense is "wholly and exclusively" for the purpose of the company's trade. This would be the case if it wasn't clear that this was part of your remuneration package.

The Taxman might be happy to include the payment of school fees as part of your remuneration package, but as earnings instead of as a benefit-in-kind. How is this possible? If the ultimate liability for school fees is with the parents (as insisted upon by the school) then the company is settling your pecuniary liability. This is earnings, not a benefit-in-kind. Big tax bill!

If there is any doubt, you're better off taking an extra dividend instead to meet the school fees (provided the company has enough post-tax (at 20%) profits to do so).

28.5.3. High-risk

A high-risk strategy here would be to pay the school fees without declaring anything to the Taxman. You will get away with paying no tax on the benefits and having the tax relief on the fees.

However, if discovered, the Taxman will hit the company with a bill for the tax and NI on the net benefits grossed up to the "salary" value. In addition, there will be the company NI bill, plus fines for incorrect P11Ds and interest for late payment. This is because it will be deemed that the company has met a personal liability of an employee.

CHAPTER 29

Personal trainers

29.1. THE EXPENSE

Joining a gym isn't cheap - it can cost anywhere between £600 and £1,000 a year. And paying £1,000 out of taxed income is the equivalent to needing an additional bonus from your company of £1,724 (£1,000/58%). So is it cheaper if the company pays for it instead?

The normal rules are that if the company pays for your subscription, e.g. to a fitness club, then you will still be taxed on the value of the subscription and the company will have to pay National Insurance (NI) at 13.8%. However, even though you may be taxed on the subscription, it could still be worth your while getting the company to pay for it. And unlike salary, you have no NI to pay.

Just the NI savings make it cheaper for your company to pay the gym membership on your behalf. But there are even greater savings to be had if it can be treated as a tax-free benefit. In simple terms, sports and recreational "facilities" can be provided tax-free if they are: **(1)** generally available to all employees; **(2)** not on domestic premises; and **(3)** not a facility available to the public generally.

T_{IP}

Rather than join a gym, why not hire a personal fitness trainer as the "sports facility"? At, say, £30 a session two days a week, that's about £240 a month tax-free. Just make sure the option of hiring the trainer is open to all employees (perhaps as part of their benefits package).

T_{IP}

If you belong to a business group, why not club together with the other members and hire a local gym or health club for exclusive use for your employees on, say, certain evenings, so excluding the members of the public at those times?

T_{IP}

If the expense is part of your remuneration package with your company, then it's generally tax deductible for it as part of staff costs. So why not have a personal trainer as part of that package? This is cheaper for you and is deductible for your company.

29.2. WHAT ARE THE POTENTIAL TAX SAVINGS?

If you pay for a personal fitness trainer out of your own money, then it's likely to be income that's already suffered tax. If it's income from your company, this money has probably been extracted as either salary or dividends. If you can reduce your tax bill by getting the company to pay direct then you are in a winning situation. So what could be the potential tax savings?

EXAMPLE

One of your directors wishes to hire a personal trainer at a cost of £600 a year. As the director is a higher rate taxpayer, he would have to receive extra salary of £1,034 (600/58%) to provide the equivalent benefit and the company would have to pay £143 (1,034 x 13.8%) NI on this extra salary. However, by the company contracting for the £600 direct, it pays NI of only £83 (£600 x 13.8%) and the director pays tax of £240. And, unlike salary, the director has no NI to pay.

TIP

To get the NI savings, make sure the company contracts directly with the personal trainer. If you pay first and then the company reimburses you, this will be treated as additional salary and any potential tax savings will be lost.

29.2.1. Corporation Tax

Your company will get a tax deduction for the expenditure itself and the employers' NI on your benefit-in-kind. You would not get a tax deduction. This leaves more money in the company for you to take out at a later stage. **Rule of thumb.** The company will save Corporation Tax on this benefit-in-kind (net of VAT) at the rate of 20%. You will save employees' NI at the rate of either 12% or 2%.

29.3. THE PAPERWORK

You've reassessed your remuneration package to include a personal fitness trainer as a benefit-in-kind for yourself. What your company needs to do is put this arrangement in writing - both amongst the company board minutes and as an addition to your contract of employment.

Your company will have to get its external reporting right both in its accounts and to the Taxman as part of its annual expenses and benefits reporting (P11Ds etc.).

29.3.1. The board minute

In your board minute you could even add a commercial reason for the company agreeing to include the personal trainer arrangement as part of your remuneration package.

The company is concerned at the lack of energy being displayed by its employees. As from November 30 2011, the company will contract and pay for a personal trainer to be available to all staff, subject to a maximum consultation of five hours a week for each employee. Consultations to take place outside of office hours in the employee's own time. This benefit-in-kind is from that date part of their remuneration package with the company and will be provided subject to the company having sufficient funds to do so. The impact of this fit-for-work campaign will be reviewed at the end of twelve months.

You're not trying to hide anything from the Taxman; in fact you want this out in the open and agreed.

TIP

Write to your advisor telling them what you're thinking of doing so that it can eventually be included on your P11D.

29.3.2. Your contract of employment

If you can't get a tax exemption making the personal trainer available to all staff (including you), then your company needs to include this benefit as an addition to your remuneration package.

EXAMPLE

Amendment to contract of employment:

"As from November 30 2011, the company will contract and pay for a personal trainer to be available to you, subject to a maximum consultation of five hours a week out of normal office hours. This benefit-in-kind is from that date and this part of your remuneration package with the company will be provided by it subject to the company having sufficient funds to do so."

29.3.3. Contract with/invoice from the supplier

You need the personal trainer's services to be treated as a benefit-in-kind. Any contract with a fitness guru needs to be negotiated by, addressed to and clearly seen to be a liability of the company.

29.3.4. On the VAT return

As long as the "personal trainer" facility is made available to all employees, the company can recover the VAT.

29.3.5. On your P11D

Your company needs to enter the VAT-inclusive cost(s) (even if the company has already claimed the VAT) of the personal trainer on your own P11D. This is if you haven't been able to use the "available to all employees" get out clause.

29.3.6. In the company's accounts

Book the cost of this "fit for work" initiative to "staff costs". This reinforces your company's argument that it is part of a remuneration package and hence it can claim a tax deduction for it.

29.3.7. Your tax return

You simply take the figure given to you by the company for your P11D benefit and put it on your tax return. No further disclosures are required by you.

29.4.   LOW, MEDIUM AND HIGH-RISK STRATEGIES

29.4.1. Low-risk

The company can pay but make sure that the personal trainer facility is open to all employees.

29.4.2. Medium-risk

The company does not get a tax deduction for the costs of a personal trainer because the Taxman doesn't accept that this expense is "wholly and exclusively" for the purpose of the company's trade. This would be the case if it wasn't clear that this was part of your company's policy towards all staff.

29.4.3. High-risk

You keep the personal trainer all to yourself but claim the tax exemption (and hence no P11D reporting) as if it were available to all staff. You now wait six years and hope the Taxman doesn't pick this up before then. If he does, there will be the overdue tax, interest and penalties to pay.

CHAPTER 30

Cars for the family

30.1. THE EXPENSE

Let's say that one of your dependants needs a car but they cannot afford the cost of running it. They don't work for your company and so wouldn't be entitled to a company car in their own right. You would like to help but if you give them the money it will be after you have paid tax and NI at, say, 41%, which makes it an expensive option for you.

In these circumstances it might be tax-effective for you to have two company cars but let them use one. If a second company-owned car is made available for private use as part of your remuneration package, the company can pay for all the repairs, running costs and even the insurance and claim Corporation Tax relief on these expenses as well as on the car itself. The catch is a benefit-in-kind charge on you for a second car. So how much tax will this cost you?

30.2. WHAT IT MIGHT COST

The taxable benefit of company cars is based on their CO_2 emissions. The lower the figure, the lower the percentage of list price used to calculate the taxable benefit. It starts at 15% for cars up to 125g/km and increases by 1% for each 5g/km thereafter up to a 35% maximum. However, from April 6 2011 a surcharge of 3% applies to all diesels (including type L diesels approved to Euro IV emissions limits and first registered before January 1 2006).

EXAMPLE

If your company buys, say, a car with a list price £10,000 (which has CO_2 emissions of 135g/km) and makes this available for private use by your son or daughter, the tax cost to you as an extra benefit-in-kind would be £10,000 x17% = £1,700 taxable on you at 40% = £680. That's the cost of the car plus all its running costs for just under £700. The savings can be greater for more expensive cars.

TIP

If the second car arrives as a present in, say, October 2011, the tax cost for 2011/12 will be even less because the car will have only been available for just six months of the tax year.

The company will also have to pay employers' NI at 13.8% on the value of this car benefit. In our example this would be £235 (£1,700 x 13.8%).

30.3.   WHAT ARE THE POTENTIAL TAX SAVINGS?

Obviously, your company has to pay the financing and running costs of the car. However, this is going to work out cheaper from a tax point of view than drawing the money out of your company, paying tax on that and using the net of tax amount to fund the car personally.

Changes from 2011/12

There have been some changes to the car benefit rules for 2011/2 which might affect the tax you pay on your company car. From April 6 2011:

- there is no longer any reduction for alternative fuels (hybrids, bi-fuels and cars manufactured to run on E85 - types H, B and G)

- the diesel surcharge of 3% applies to all diesels (including type L diesels approved to Euro IV emissions limits and first registered before January 1 2006)

- the £80,000 limit for the price of a car for car benefit purposes no longer applies

- the lower threshold (the CO_2 emissions figure which sets the 15% rate) has been reduced from 130 to 125g/km.

Looking ahead to 20012/13 the changes that have currently been announced are:

- the special rules for QUALECs (qualifying low emissions cars, those with CO_2 emissions not exceeding exactly 120g/km) will be abolished

- the lowest appropriate percentage will still be 10%, but will apply to cars with CO_2 emissions of up to 99g/km. The rate for emissions of 100g/km will be 11% and will increase by 1% for every 5g/km to the current maximum of 35%, as at present.

30.4.   THE PAPERWORK

To avoid any quibble with the Taxman, have this second car recorded as part of your remuneration package with the company. It's tax deductible for the company "wholly and exclusively" to keep its key member of staff (you) happy.

You've reassessed your remuneration package to include in it a second company car as a benefit-in-kind for yourself. What your company needs to do is put this arrangement in writing - both amongst the company board minutes and as an addition to your contract of employment.

Once the car has been acquired, your company then has to get its external reporting right, first by notifying the Taxman of a new company car and secondly by calculating the benefit-in-kind on its P11D.

30.4.1. The board minute

In your board minute include a commercial reason for the company agreeing to add a second company car to your remuneration package.

EXAMPLE

The board minute covering the second car could read as follows:

"In recognition of your contribution to the company and to avoid sharing your company car with other members of your family, the company has decided that as part of your remuneration package, it will make available for your private use a second company car. This is, of course, subject to the company being able to finance both the acquisition cost and running expenses of this second vehicle."

You're not trying to hide anything from the Taxman; in fact you want this out in the open and agreed.

TIP

Write to your advisor telling them what you're doing so that it can be included on your P11D.

30.4.2. Your contract of employment

Your company needs to put this addition to your remuneration package in writing as an amendment to your contract of employment.

EXAMPLE

Amendment to contract of employment:

"As from November 30 2011, the company will make available to you a second company car. This benefit-in-kind is from that date part of your remuneration package with the company and will be provided by it subject to the company being able to finance both the acquisition cost and running expenses."

30.4.3. Notifying the Taxman of an additional car

To add credibility to the company's planned intention to provide you with a second company car, send in a completed P46 (Car) Form to the Taxman.

30.4.4. On your P11D

Your company needs to disclose the taxable benefit figure for both cars on your P11D, which has to be submitted to the Taxman by July 6 each year.

30.4.5. Your tax return

You simply take the figure given to you by the company for your P11D benefit (for both company cars) and put this on your tax return. No further disclosures are required by you.

30.5. LOW, MEDIUM AND HIGH-RISK STRATEGIES

30.5.1. Low-risk

If you get the paperwork right, the low-risk strategy is the one outlined above.

30.5.2. Medium-risk

The company won't get a tax deduction for the cost of your second company car because the Taxman doesn't accept that this expense is "wholly and exclusively" for the purpose of the company's trade. This would be the case if it wasn't clear that this was part of your remuneration package.

30.5.3. High-risk

You put the second company car down as a pool car - but it isn't! You wait six years and hope the Taxman doesn't pick this up before then. If he does, there will be the overdue tax, interest and penalties to pay.

CHAPTER 31

Company plane (or yacht)

31.1. THE EXPENSE

Many of us are frustrated jet setters. We would love, but can't afford, to own and run a yacht or private plane. Is there a way that a company could pay for this instead?

Here, we'll concentrate on a company plane but the Taxman's view is broadly the same for boats. If your existing company just bought an aircraft and you had sole/exclusive use of it, then you would be taxed on a benefit-in-kind calculated at 20% of the annual "value" of that plane. This will be calculated by the inspector as *"total flying hours times the most expensive commercial hire rate"* he can find. So what you should do is…

Step 1

Purchase a light aircraft via a limited company (specifically formed for that purpose) of which you are the sole director/shareholder, using a mortgage secured on the aircraft. Then...

Step 2

Hire out the aircraft to commercial operators - who will use it for commercial operations such as training. Why do this? You are telling the Taxman that the company's objective is to hire out the plane commercially in order to repay the borrowings. It's not a hobby!

> **TIP**
>
> For the benefit of the Taxman prepare some figures showing expected (monthly) cash flows in and out to support your intentions. This should show that the company can repay the mortgage and make a modest profit right from the outset.

Step 3

Draft an agreement between yourself (as a director) and the company specifying that you can only use it on a commercial basis at an agreed rate per hour.

You now don't have exclusive use of the plane, so the Taxman can't use his figures. Instead, you agree with him some form of (lower) hourly rate for private use. So how is this done?

The hourly rate for private use could be *"total expenses times the number of hours flown by you/total hours"*. Total expenses will be in your company's accounts at the end of the year. The name of the game here is to maximise total hours.

Total hours will include: **(1)** earning time - hours flown by the customers; **(2)** private use - hours flown by you for pleasure; **(3)** positioning and exercise - flights to place the aircraft where it is needed for hiring or just to turn the engine and prevent static decay; **(4)** servicing - hours in the workshop; and **(5)** idle time - aircraft fully available but unused.

Go to the Taxman with the rate you have calculated and get it agreed before you have to put it on the P11D. This way you avoid any penalties.

TIP

Charge your other business a fee for using the plane as transport for business trips. Increasingly, planes are used for business trips by busy executives in place of our choked road system. What the Taxman can't do is disallow expenses in your other company on the grounds that you have not taken the cheapest transport option.

Don't think that our advice is limited to planes. Anything that you are interested in can be treated in the same way - if it could be hired out commercially. So why not sign up for that course of flying or sailing lessons? Clever tax treatment of what you are doing could help turn your dreams into reality.

31.2. WHAT ARE THE POTENTIAL TAX SAVINGS?

If you buy and run a plane with your own resources, then they're likely to have come from income that has already suffered tax. If it's income from your company, this money has probably been extracted as either salary or dividends. If you can reduce your tax bill by getting the company to pay direct, then you are in a winning situation. So what are the potential tax savings?

The savings come from establishing that the opportunity with the plane is a business not a personal hobby. The way of getting business status for a plane would be to set up a chartering company. The fact that it might be chartered on occasion to you, as the business owner, shouldn't prevent this, provided you are not the only charterer. If you are going to go down this road, make sure you can demonstrate that you are adopting a 100% business-like approach to the purchase. Ideally you should create and document a fully worked out business plan, and you should be able to demonstrate that you have tried as hard as you can to secure charters.

If the plane is acquired on finance, business treatment enables you to claim the interest element of the finance against tax.

If you are using the plane as the fixed asset of a business, capital allowances are available against the income from the business activity. Capital allowances are the tax equivalent of depreciation and are designed, over the life of the asset, to write off all of its cost against income.

Benefit-in-kind trap

EXAMPLE

You manage to find third party charters for the company plane for 20 weeks of the year, and use it yourself for three weeks. Instead of what you would probably regard as fair, that is a benefit-in-kind charge of 3/23 of the cost of providing the plane, you could end up with 32/52 of the costs as a benefit, on the basis that, all the time it was not being chartered by others, it was "available" for your use.

TIP

Establish that the plane is not available to you at times when you are not using it. A board minute and actual use that complies with it should be effective in reducing the benefit-in-kind charge.

31.3. THE PAPERWORK

As we have said already, the tax advantages depend on being able to successfully claim some kind of "business" status for the plane.

If you only want that plane for private use, how can you pretend that it is a business asset? Well, there is certainly no question of pretending anything; valid tax planning has to be on the basis of full disclosure and none of our advice depends on deceiving the Taxman or anyone else.

31.3.1. Projected cash flow and profit and loss

Prepare some figures showing expected (monthly) cash flows in and out to support your intentions. This should show that the company can fund any loan secured on the plane and make a modest profit right from the outset.

31.3.2. Agreement between you and the company

Have a formal written agreement between yourself and the company specifying that you can only use the plane on a commercial basis at an agreed rate per hour.

Company plane (or yacht)

31.3.3. The board minute

Have a board minute on file agreeing to your use of the plane but on a restricted basis.

You're not trying to hide anything from the Taxman; in fact, you want this out in the open and agreed.

31.3.4. On your P11D

If the hourly rate for private use per your agreement with the company is *"total expenses x number of hours flown by you/ total hours"*, you will need a record on your P11D file of: **(1)** an analysis of the plane's total costs (including VAT); and **(2)** total hours, broken down into the components outlined above (from the plane's own log book).

Your company then needs to enter the value of "private hours x agreed rate per hour" in the tax year on your P11D.

31.3.5. Your tax return

You simply take the figure given to you by the company for your P11D benefit and put it on your tax return. No further disclosures are required by you.

31.4. LOW, MEDIUM AND HIGH-RISK STRATEGIES

31.4.1. Low-risk

If you get the paperwork right, the low-risk strategy is the one outlined above.

So why not sign up for that course of flying or sailing lessons and make a note of the date of the next boat show? Clever tax treatment of what you are doing could help turn your dreams into reality.

31.4.2. Medium-risk

You forget to draft an agreement between yourself and the company specifying that you can only use it on a commercial basis at an agreed rate per hour. If the Taxman asks for a copy of the agreement and you can't produce one, he'll tax you on the plane being available to you for the whole year! Ouch.

You now don't have exclusive use of the plane, so the Taxman can't assess you with a full year's benefit-in-kind.

31.4.3. High-risk

You don't bother with a separate company and buy it with funds in your existing business. There's no real prospect of external chartering, no agreement between you and your company and it ends up being your exclusive plane. The Taxman picks out this large addition to fixed assets and opens an enquiry into all aspects of your existing company's affairs not just the plane perk! Or you get lucky and he doesn't spot anything for six years.

Company plane (or yacht)

CHAPTER 32

Gym membership

32.1. THE EXPENSE

If the company meets the personal expenditure of a director or employee, the Taxman can assess the company to tax on the difference between the sum paid out and the gross salary equivalent. He'll also want NI and penalties on top. So how is it that you can get your gym membership paid for by the company without being penalised in this way and what are the savings that can be made?

32.2. WHAT ARE THE POTENTIAL TAX SAVINGS?

If you pay for your membership yourself, it will come from income that's already had tax deducted from it. However, if the company pays, then you save some of the tax that you would have paid on that income withdrawal. The potential savings are examined below.

32.2.1. Savings on your salary

If the company pays for your membership fees, it will be treated as a benefit-in-kind and taxable on you as the director/employee, based on the amount paid.

The tax on this will be less than the amount you would have had to take in salary to pay your membership. In addition, there won't be any employees' NI to pay either. The company will pay NI, but once again it will be on a lesser amount than the salary equivalent.

32.2.2. Corporation Tax

Your company will get a tax deduction for all the cost of the gym membership. In addition, the NI paid by the company on the value of the benefit-in-kind gets tax relief. This means there's more money left in the company for you to take at a later date.

32.3. EXAMPLE

Let's say your annual gym membership fees for you and your family are £1,500. This is the amount you would need after tax and NI has been deducted by the company. We can now compare the relative tax positions if the £1,500 is treated as net salary or a benefit-in-kind.

32.3.1. You

	40% TAXPAYER (£)
Tax and NI on salary £1,500 x 42/58)	1,086
Tax on benefits of £1,500	486
Saving	442

32.3.2. Your company and NI

	40% TAXPAYER (£)
Ers' NI on salary @13.8%	357
Ers' NI on benefits of £1,500@13.8%	207
Saving	150

32.3.3. Corporation Tax saving on a benefit

	£
Corporation Tax on annual subscription (£1,500 @ 20%)	300
Corporation Tax on employers' NI (£207 @ 20%)	41
Saving	341

32.4. THE PAPERWORK

By taking the following steps you will be making sure that there is no room for a challenge by the Taxman. And with all the paperwork done correctly there should be no risk of penalties arising at a later date either.

32.4.1. The board minute

Remember, any expense charged in the company's accounts has to meet the "wholly and exclusively" test. Getting a formal board minute drawn up demonstrates to the Taxman that the benefit was agreed on by the company as a way of rewarding you for your services to the company. There is no need for any special wording, just a statement of the facts as a record for future reference.

EXAMPLE

"Meeting of the Board of Directors of XYZ Limited on .... at ...

It was resolved that the company approve the payment of an annual subscription to .... as part of their remuneration package.

This award has been made in recognition of their continuing contribution to the success of the company.

Signed .... company secretary."

32.4.2. Contract of employment

Because this is a variation of your remuneration package you will need to incorporate it into your contract of employment by way of an addendum.

"as of .... the company will pay your membership of .... This benefit-in-kind is to be treated as part of your remuneration package with the company."

32.4.3. Contract with/invoice from the supplier

Getting the supplier to invoice the company will make it absolutely clear that the liability for payment belongs with the company and not you.

32.4.4. On the VAT return

As the contract is with the company, any VAT charged on the membership fees can be reclaimed on your company's VAT return.

32.4.5. On your P11D

The value of the benefit-in-kind to be included is the total cost of the membership before the deduction of VAT.

32.4.6. In the company's accounts

Although there are no special disclosure requirements, if you include the charge for the cost of the gym membership as part of "remuneration costs", it reinforces your position that it's part of your pay package.

32.4.7. On your tax return

Simply transfer the values from your P11D to the relevant boxes on your tax return's employment pages. Any tax due will then be collected in the normal way.

32.5. LOW, MEDIUM AND HIGH-RISK STRATEGIES

32.5.1. Low-risk

Getting the paperwork right as described above cuts all risk down to an absolute minimum.

32.5.2. Medium-risk

If it's unclear that the payment is part of your remuneration package, there's a risk that the company won't be allowed a deduction in the accounts under the "true and fair" rules. This means a loss of Corporation Tax relief.

32.5.3. High-risk

A high-risk strategy here would be for your company to pay for your gym membership without declaring any benefit to you personally. However, if discovered, the Taxman will hit the company with a bill for the tax and NI on the payment grossed up to the "salary" value because the company has met a personal liability of the employee.

CHAPTER 33

Garage storage

33.1. THE EXPENSE

A colleague has told you that they charge their company rent for the use of their garage - presumably just to keep their company car in out of the rain. What's the full story here and is this really something you could take advantage of?

The Taxman say's that any allowance paid to an employee for keeping a company vehicle in the employee's own garage will be taxable. In such a case, PAYE needs to be applied - meaning the payment is treated as net salary and then grossed up to work out the tax and NI due. This applies whether or not the garage is attached to your residence. So it doesn't look as if your colleague is telling the full story. However, there are a couple of loopholes that you might be able to exploit.

Protecting the company car

The Taxman's manual refers to circumstances in which the employer requires the employee to rent a garage for a vehicle owned by the employer and accepts that there is no benefit to the employee in these circumstances, even if the cost of renting the garage is paid by the employee and reimbursed by the employer.

> EXAMPLE
>
> David's house has no garage, so consequently, cars are parked on the road. A garage recently became available nearby and he arranged for the company to rent this and the car is now kept there overnight and during other periods when it is not being used.

There is no specification as to how much rent you are allowed to claim or how big (other than car size) the garage should be. Just don't go over the top. The key thing is that you must not own the garage.

Storeroom, not garage

Let's say, for example, that you use your garage to store product samples for your company. Is it possible to claim some expenses in addition to the rent claimed for using your home as an office?

You'll always need to work hard to convince the Taxman on anything to do with your home. But if you use part of your home for the duties of your employment (for example, because you live and work some distance from your head office), you can claim the additional cost of working from home. If you have a homeworking agreement with your company in place, it can pay you a minimum of £3 a week tax-free to cover these additional costs. However, any allowance paid to you for use of your garage normally counts as earnings. Therefore, PAYE should be applied to the payment. This will be the case whether or not the garage is attached to your home.

However, where an employer claims that the payment to an employee is rent chargeable on the employee as property income, then this is tax deductible for the company and not earnings of the employee. So all you need to do is charge your company rent for the use of your garage.

33.2. THE PAPERWORK

By taking the following steps you will be making sure that there is no room for a challenge by the Taxman. And with all the paperwork completed correctly there should be no risk of penalties arising at a later date either.

Protecting the company car

Get a letter from your company insisting that the car is locked in a garage overnight "for security reasons". There should also be reference in the letter to the fact that you will be reimbursed for the additional costs involved in this garaging. The company should also approach its tax office to inform the Taxman why it considers no entry on a P11D is needed for this specific expense payment and requesting agreement to this. It's easier to get this agreed right from the start rather than several years later during a routine PAYE inspection visit.

Storeroom, not garage

Alternatively, record any payment to you by your company for use of your garage as rent, both in your company's books as an expense and on your own tax return as income. However, on your return you now get to claim for any additional costs of meeting your company's requirements for the safe keeping etc. of that stock whilst it's in your garage.

33.2.1. Rental agreement

Back up this storeroom payment with a licence agreement between you and your company setting out the terms and conditions of the rental agreement. Include the additional measures your company expects you to take over preserving the condition of the stock.

EXAMPLE

- the property owners to take such steps as are necessary for the items stored not to be exposed to high or low temperatures whilst within the garage storage
- the property owners to put suitable security and fire prevention measures in place to reduce the risk of loss of items held in the garage storage
- the property owners to put such procedures in place that will allow the garage storage to comply with the Company's health and safety policy.

33.2.2. On the VAT return

There's no VAT involved in this expense.

33.2.3. On your P11D

No entry required.

33.2.4. In the company's accounts

Although there are no special disclosure requirements, if you include the payment for rent under "rent and rates", it reinforces your position that it's that type of business expense.

33.2.5. On your tax return

You'll need to record the rent you receive from your company as rental income on your tax return. Remember to claim the costs of supplying this facility to your company (in line with any specific requirements it might have).

33.3. LOW, MEDIUM AND HIGH-RISK STRATEGIES

33.3.1. Low-risk

Getting the paperwork right as described above cuts all risk down to an absolute minimum.

TIP

If you already claim "use of home as office", include the garage as an additional room for apportioning costs between business and non-business. Plus claim for costs directly related to providing that storage.

33.3.2. Medium-risk

If it's unclear that the payment is rent, there's a risk that it will be treated as net salary and the Taxman will come looking for tax and NI on the gross equivalent.

33.3.3. High-risk

You pay yourself a round sum allowance from the company for the privilege of parking your company car in your own garage. If discovered, the Taxman will want to treat this as net salary that needs grossing up for unpaid Tax and NI. There will also be interest and penalties.

CHAPTER 34

Nannies

34.1.   THE EXPENSE

Unfortunately, hiring a nanny to provide additional childcare in your own home comes with a tax cost. As a general rule, if an employee such as a nanny earns more than (currently) £136 a week you have to operate a payroll for them. This means working out how much income tax and NI is due on their wages/salary and paying this across to the Taxman on a regular basis.

If you engage a nanny through an agency, they would deal with all the PAYE etc. for you. But you would probably end up paying more as the agency builds its own profit margin into the going rate for nannies.

Can't you just put the nanny onto your company's payroll instead of employing them yourself? We don't recommend this, even though it may save on agency fees. The Taxman's view is that the full cost of the nanny's wages plus employers' NI is treated as your extra salary. You can't even offset the tax and NI already paid by the nanny through the payroll against your own surprise tax bill.

34.2.   WHAT IT MIGHT COST

34.2.1. If you directly employ a nanny

EXAMPLE

Nanny is paid £15,000 a year by the Darling family to look after their children. She would be paid less if she lived with the family but she chooses to have her own accommodation (lives out). On top of the salary the family has to pay employers' NI of £976 p.a. ((£15,000 - £7,072 NI free) x 13.8%).

From Nanny's salary the Darlings have to deduct a total of £933 in employees' NI and £1,505 in income tax and pay it over to the Taxman - together with the employers' NI. This leaves Nanny with an after tax salary of £12,562 (just over £1,050 per month).

34.2.2. As a benefit-in-kind from your company

EXAMPLE

Your company engages an agency to provide the nanny as part of your remuneration package. On a cost to the company of £18,000 (£15,000 plus VAT) you, as a 40% taxpayer, will pay income tax of £7,200 - even though the company is able to claim back the VAT through its VAT return. Your company's employers' Class 1A NI bill on this benefit-in-kind (including VAT) is £2,484 (£18,000x 13.8%). However, the Corporation Tax deduction is worth £3,672 (£15,000 + £2,484 = £17,484 at, say, 20%).

34.3. WHAT ARE THE POTENTIAL TAX SAVINGS?

If you pay the nanny yourself, it will come from income that's already had tax deducted from it. However, if the company pays, then you save some of the tax that you would have paid on that income withdrawal.

As part of your remuneration package, your company will get a tax deduction for the cost of providing the nanny. You can't claim a tax deduction for the nanny through your own tax return. And this means there's more money left in the company for you to take at a later date.

34.4. THE PAPERWORK

By taking the following steps you will be making sure that there is no room for a challenge by the Taxman. And with all the paperwork completed correctly there should be no risk of penalties arising at a later date either.

34.4.1. The board minute

Remember, any expense charged in the company's accounts has to meet the "wholly and exclusively" test. Getting a formal board minute drawn up demonstrates to the Taxman that the benefit was agreed on by the company as a way of rewarding you for your services to the company. There is no need for any special wording, just a statement of the facts as a record for future reference.

EXAMPLE

"Meeting of the Board of Directors of XYZ Limited on .... at ....

It was resolved that the company approve the engagement of a nanny (through an agency) as part of ...... 's remuneration package.

This award has been made in recognition of their continuing contribution to the success of the company.

Signed .... company secretary."

34.4.2. Contract of employment

Because this is a variation of your remuneration package you will need to incorporate it into your contract of employment by way of an addendum.

EXAMPLE

"as of .... the company will engage a nanny (through an agency). This benefit-in-kind is to be treated as part of your remuneration package with the company."

34.4.3. Contract with/invoice from the supplier

Getting the supplier to invoice the company will make it absolutely clear that the liability for payment belongs with the company and not you.

34.4.4. On the VAT return

As the contract is with the company, any VAT charged by the nanny's agency can be reclaimed on your company's VAT return.

34.4.5. On your P11D

The value of the benefit-in-kind to be included is the total cost of the nanny (including VAT).

34.4.6. In the company's accounts

Although there are no special disclosure requirements, if you include the charge for the cost of the nanny as part of "remuneration costs", it reinforces the position that it's part of your pay package.

34.4.7. On your tax return

Simply transfer the values from your P11D to the relevant boxes on your tax return's employment pages. Any tax due will then be collected in the normal way.

34.5. LOW, MEDIUM AND HIGH-RISK STRATEGIES

34.5.1. Low-risk

Getting the paperwork right as described above cuts all risk down to an absolute minimum.

34.5.2. Medium-risk

If it's unclear that the payment is part of your remuneration package, there's a risk that the company won't be allowed as a deduction in the accounts under the "true and fair" rules. This means a loss of Corporation Tax relief.

34.5.3. High-risk

A high-risk strategy here would be to use the company bank account to settle what you owe the nanny and not declare the benefit to you on your P11D. You get away with paying no tax on the benefits and your company might initially get tax relief on the cost of the agency nanny. However, if this expense distorts your company's accounts too much, this increases the chance of the Taxman opening an enquiry. If the truth is discovered, the Taxman will hit the company with a bill for the tax and NI on this expense grossed up as "salary". In addition, there will be the company NI bill, plus fines for incorrect P11Ds and interest for late payment.

CHAPTER 35

The weekend away

35.1. THE EXPENSE

Getting away from work for any reasonable length of time can be difficult. If you fancy a weekend or two away, are there ways that you can legitimately get your company to pay for them?

As a general rule, transportation costs are tax deductible if the primary purpose of your trip is business-related. So how can you take advantage of this? Say you would like to travel to the Lake District, primarily to see customers, prospects, suppliers etc. in the area. Or you're due to travel to a conference. Why not squeeze in a couple of extra days to your itinerary to get the break you deserve?

If you have business meetings on, say, Friday and Monday in a particular area, there's no need to go home for the weekend. You can spend Saturday and Sunday at, say, the nearest health spa, tennis club or cricket ground and still get a tax deduction for most of the expenses.

If you travel outside the UK, you can write off 100% of your transportation costs if your trip was primarily for business and you were outside the UK for, say, a week or less. On longer foreign trips, the Taxman will look for a business (yes) versus pleasure (no) allocation of expenses.

Investigate where conferences for your industry or profession are being held. See if these coincide with your choice of a nice location for a weekend break, or even just a hotel that has it all. The trip must be seen to be primarily for business for your travel expenses to be deductible along with most, if not all, of your hotel bills.

Your company can claim a full tax deduction for the cost of genuine business travel, related hotel accommodation and subsistence. However, there is a condition - the costs must be incurred "wholly exclusively and necessarily for the furtherance of the trade". So with our weekend break plan, your travel and accommodation costs should be deductible - what you choose to do in the hours when not attending clients is none of the Taxman's business.

EXAMPLE

You take a four-day business trip. After four days of work-related appointments, you spend two days at the same hotel, swimming and sightseeing. Because you devoted more time to business than pleasure, your travel will be deductible. Other outlays (hotels, meals etc.) may be written off by your company for the business-related portion of the trip.

TIP

Keep a log to show that the key days were focused on business. Retain copies of pre-trip correspondence arranging meetings, agendas for the conference, and post-trip follow-ups.

Companion

For you to deduct the travel costs of a spouse or significant other, your companion must be an employee of the company, with a business purpose for going along. However, even if your companion has no business purpose for being there, their attendance doesn't disqualify your business trip. Of course, if they meet their own (additional) expenses, then there's no real tax issue here. If their bills end up on your company credit card, the best way to solve this is to write the company a personal cheque to cover them.

Finally, any of the expenses incurred by your spouse/partner will be deductible if you incur them yourself and just share the benefits with them, e.g. taxi fares, car rental etc.

35.2. WHAT ARE THE POTENTIAL TAX SAVINGS?

If you pay for the whole trip yourself, it will come from income that's already had tax deducted from it. However, if the company pays, then you save some of the tax that you would have paid on that income withdrawal. Your company will be permitted to make a deduction in its accounts for the business element of the trip, which means it pays less Corporation Tax.

35.3. THE PAPERWORK

By taking the following steps you will be making sure that there is no room for a challenge by the Taxman. And with all the paperwork done correctly there should be no risk of penalties arising at a later date either.

35.3.1. The board minute

Remember, any expense charged in the company's accounts has to meet the "wholly and exclusively" test. Getting a formal board minute drawn up demonstrates to the Taxman that the trip was agreed on by the company for a commercial reason. There is no need for any special wording, just a statement of the facts as a record for future reference.

EXAMPLE

A director decided to take an extended trip to visit suppliers, and to take his wife, Jeanette, with him. Before booking the tickets, he called a board meeting at which it was resolved that *"Jeanette be asked to accompany John in order to assist him at social engagements for the benefit of the company's business"*. The company secretary (who just happens to be Jeanette) also recorded in the minutes that the board thought that her presence produced minimal additional expenditure.

35.3.2. Invoices

Hotel bills etc. should be addressed to the company rather than yourself. In fact, it's probably best to get as much of the trip paid for via the company credit/debit card as possible.

35.3.3. On the VAT return

You can make a reasonable apportionment of VAT between business and non-business purposes if the expenses include a private element.

35.3.4. On your P11D

There will be no entries on your P11D for this trip if you reimburse any private element to the expenses.

35.3.5. In the company's accounts

There are no special disclosure requirements, just include the costs of the trip within "travel costs".

35.3.6. Your tax return

Simply transfer the values from your P11D to the relevant boxes on your tax return's employment pages. Any tax due will then be collected in the normal way.

35.4. LOW, MEDIUM AND HIGH-RISK STRATEGIES

35.4.1. Low-risk

If you get the paperwork right, the low-risk strategy is the one outlined above. Add holiday days to a business trip, as practically all costs associated with making that trip are tax deductible. Remember to make a contribution to the resultant company credit card bill for the non-business element.

35.4.2. Medium-risk

The company does not get a tax deduction for the trip because the Taxman doesn't accept that this expense is "wholly and exclusively" for the purpose of the company's trade. This would be the case if it wasn't clear that you had reimbursed the company for any private costs and that the private benefit from the trip as a whole was merely incidental.

35.4.3. High-risk

A high-risk strategy here would be to get the company to pay for the whole cost of the trip without declaring any private element to the Taxman. You will get away with paying no tax on the benefits and your company having the tax relief on the costs. However, if discovered, the Taxman will hit the company with a bill for the tax and NI on private expenses. In addition, the company will have fines for incorrect returns and interest for late payment of tax underpaid. This is because it will be deemed that the company has met a personal liability of an employee.

CHAPTER 36

Domestic help

36.1. THE EXPENSE

You're so busy with your company that some of those domestic household chores aren't getting done as regularly as they might be. So paying for someone to come in and help with the cleaning, ironing, etc. is a useful option. It occurs to you that as it's your business that's keeping you occupied why can't it pay for this extra domestic help?

36.2. WHAT IT MIGHT COST

EXAMPLE

Your company pays £40 every fortnight for two 1½ hour cleaning sessions a week at your home. It uses a firm which provides the cleaning materials etc. and also has insurance cover for their staff whilst in your home, including accidental damage clauses. It pays that firm's invoice rather than give you cash to leave for the cleaning staff.

36.3. WHAT ARE THE POTENTIAL TAX SAVINGS?

If you pay for the domestic help out of your own pocket, then it's likely to be from income that has already suffered tax. If it's income from your company, this money has probably been extracted as either salary or dividends. If you can reduce your tax bill by getting the company to pay direct, then you are in a winning situation.

36.4. THE PAPERWORK

You've reassessed your remuneration package to include a domestic help expense you would like the company to incur as a benefit-in-kind. What your company needs to do is put this arrangement in writing - both amongst the company board minutes and as an addition to your contract of employment.

Once the domestic help has been completed your company then has to get its external reporting right, first to the VATman, then in its accounts and finally to the Taxman on its P11D.

36.4.1. The board minute

If you go down the benefit-in-kind route, your company's board minutes should include a commercial reason for the company agreeing to include domestic cleaning arrangements as part of your remuneration package.

EXAMPLE

The board minute covering domestic help in Jim's home reads as follows:

"In recognition of your contribution to the company and to spend more time on company business each week, the company has decided that as part of your remuneration package it will contract and pay for domestic help for two mornings a week at your principal private residence. This is of course subject to the company having sufficient funds to do so."

You're not trying to hide anything from the Taxman; in fact, you want this out in the open and agreed.

TIP

Write to your advisor telling them what you're planning on doing so that it can be included on your P11D.

36.4.2. Your contract of employment

Your company needs to put this addition to your remuneration package in writing as an amendment to your contract of employment.

EXAMPLE

Amendment to contract of employment:

"As from November 30 2011, the company will contract and pay for domestic help for two mornings a week at your principal private residence. This benefit-in-kind is from that date part of your remuneration package with the company and will be provided by it subject to the company having sufficient funds to do so."

36.4.3. Contract with/invoice from the supplier

You need the domestic help service to be treated as a benefit-in-kind. As such the contract needs to be negotiated by, addressed to and be clearly a liability of the company.

36.4.4. On the VAT return

Most domestic cleaning outfits don't charge VAT, so nothing to take account of here.

36.4.5. On your P11D

Your company needs to enter on your P11D the cost to it of providing you with domestic help as a benefit-in-kind during the tax year.

36.4.6. In the company's accounts

Transfer the cost of this work out of "office cleaning costs" and into "staff costs". This reinforces your company's argument that it is part of your remuneration package and hence it can claim a tax deduction for it.

36.4.7. Your tax return

You simply take the figure given to you by the company for your P11D benefit and put it on your tax return. No further disclosures are required by you.

36.5. LOW, MEDIUM AND HIGH-RISK STRATEGIES

36.5.1. Low-risk

If you get the paperwork right, the low-risk strategy is the one outlined above.

36.5.2. Medium-risk

The company does not get a tax deduction for the costs of domestic help because the Taxman doesn't accept that this expense is "wholly and exclusively" for the purpose of the company's trade. This would be the case if it wasn't clear that this was part of your remuneration package.

36.5.3. High-risk

Your company enters into one contract with your office cleaning company. Their invoice is made out for one amount that includes work at all locations (including your home).

Since there is only one invoice it's going to be difficult for anyone to decide on the private amount. You wait six years and hope the Taxman doesn't pick this up before then. If he does, there will be the overdue tax, interest and penalties to pay.

CHAPTER 37

Use of the company villa

37.1. THE EXPENSE

Let's say your company decides to invest in holiday property, the main purpose being to reward key customers with free accommodation. It would need to specify the days the customer can have and (to save on your costs) make it clear they have to arrange their own transport, flights etc. The property is then available for you to use personally at other times.

The full annual running costs of the property would be deductible against the profits of the company if it actually benefits the business, i.e. through increased sales. So it would need to keep records of who uses the accommodation and when. Relate this to individual sales and you can easily show the Taxman how the business has benefited from owning the property.

Although your company doesn't get annual tax allowances on the cost of the property itself, the original cost is tax deductible when your company comes to sell the accommodation. Any taxable profit on the sale would be subject to Corporation Tax.

Location

Does the Taxman mind where the company has this property? He would be suspicious at first of a holiday villa in, say, Spain. But Mr Taxman, to make the offer attractive there is no point in having one week in a cottage in Cornwall - most people would want the same week during the summer when it might not rain. So that is why the company owns a villa in Spain. There is also the ready availability of cheap flights to Spain that make it an attractive destination for customers.

Own use

You can use the accommodation yourself but there is a tax cost to this. Even if you or your fellow directors only use, for example, a company villa for a couple of weeks a year, the Taxman will try and say that it is available to you for the whole year and tax you on its annual value.

> **TIP**
>
> Have a policy of restricting the use of the villa to a maximum number of weeks for each director. Document these restrictions in board minutes and letters to the directors. Then back this up with a record of when the visits occurred. This will not eliminate the taxable benefit but will severely restrict the Taxman's ability to assess you for tax on it.

37.2. WHAT IT MIGHT COST

If your existing company just bought a villa and you had sole/exclusive use of it, then you would be taxed on a benefit-in-kind calculated at 20% of the annual "value" of that accommodation. This will be calculated by the Taxman as the most expensive value he can find.

EXAMPLE

Customers occupy the company villa in Spain for 30 weeks of the year, but you use it yourself for three weeks. Instead of what you would probably regard as fair, that is a benefit-in-kind charge of 3/33 thirds of the cost of providing the accommodation, you could end up with 22/52 of the cost as a benefit, on the basis that all the time it was not being occupied by customers, it was "available" for your use.

You pay income tax (but no NI) and your company pays employers' class 1A NI on the value of the benefit-in-kind.

Your company has to calculate the annual value of free accommodation. The calculation of this depends on the type of property as follows:

PROPERTY	CASH EQUIVALENT VALUE
Cost less than £75,000	Gross rateable value
Cost more than £75,000	Gross rateable value plus nominal rent
Situated overseas irrespective of cost	Local market rent
Is rented by the company	Rent paid by the company
Is owned by a person connected with you and rented by the company	Market rent irrespective of the actual rent paid

You will also be taxable on a proportion of the other costs paid by the employer, e.g. telephone bills, use of furniture, appliances and repairs, internal decoration, heating, lighting and cleaning.

37.3. WHAT ARE THE POTENTIAL TAX SAVINGS?

If you pay for holiday accommodation out of your own pocket, then it's likely that this comes out of income that has already suffered tax. If it's income from your company, this money has probably been extracted as either salary or dividends. If you can reduce your tax bill by using company accommodation, then you are in a winning situation.

37.4. THE PAPERWORK

If you only want that accommodation for private use, how can you pretend that it is a business asset? Well, there's certainly no question of pretending anything, valid tax planning has to be on the basis of full disclosure and none of our advice depends on deceiving the Taxman or anyone else.

To help obtain a tax deduction for the running costs of the accommodation, what your company needs to do is record its commercial intentions right from the beginning.

It also needs to restrict the potential tax charge on you for private use of the accommodation by limiting its availability to you.

37.4.1. The board minute

The board minute covering the company's decision to acquire holiday accommodation reads as follows:

EXAMPLE

"The company has decided to invest in holiday accommodation, with the main purpose of offering this free-of-charge to customers as part of specific sales promotion campaigns. The company will retain tight control over the days the customer can have and make it clear that they have to arrange their own transport to and from the accommodation, e.g. flights. It's not the intention to use the accommodation for the provision of hospitality or entertainment generally to customers."

You're not trying to hide anything from the Taxman; in fact, you want this out in the open and agreed.

37.4.2. Marketing campaign

The full annual running costs of the property would be deductible against the profits of the company if it actually benefits the business. So keep copies of any marketing material you regularly produce using the availability of the accommodation as an incentive to lift sales.

TIP

Keep records of who uses (customers) the accommodation and when. Relate this to individual sales and you can easily show the Taxman how the business has benefited from owning the property.

37.4.3. Agreement with the company

Draft an agreement between yourself (the director) and the company specifying that you can only use the accommodation for a fixed number of weeks each year.

EXAMPLE

Private use agreement

"The company .... (insert company name)

The employee .... (insert employee name)

The employee agrees to use the .... (insert address of holiday accommodation) owned by .... (insert company name) for no more than .... (insert number of) agreed days per year. In total, the employee shall only be entitled to use it on .... (insert number) occasions per quarter.

The Company agrees to favour the employee with .... (insert number of) days for accommodation during the period of this Agreement.

Signature of employee..

Signed by (on behalf of the company) ....

Date of agreement...

I .... (insert employee name) confirm that I have read, understood and accept the Terms and Conditions of Hire."

37.4.4. Contracts with/invoices from suppliers

Contracts with local agents and other service providers for the accommodation need to be negotiated by, addressed to and be clearly a liability of the company (not yours).

37.4.5. Value of the accommodation

If situated overseas, get a local valuer to confirm in writing what rent the company's property would have obtained if it were let on the open market. This carries more weight than simply looking up ads for property rentals on the Internet.

37.4.6. VAT

The company should be able to claim back any VAT charged on the running costs of the property, but restricted to the proportion of business use to total use of the accommodation.

37.4.7. On your P11D

Your company needs to enter the benefit-in-kind figure for this free accommodation on your P11D.

37.4.8. In the company's accounts

No adjustment required to reflect the value of the benefit-in-kind.

37.4.9. Your tax return

You simply take the figure given to you by the company for your P11D benefit and put it on your tax return. No further disclosures are required by you.

37.5. LOW, MEDIUM AND HIGH-RISK STRATEGIES

37.5.1. Low-risk

If you get the paperwork right, the low-risk strategy is the one outlined above.

37.5.2. Medium-risk

The company does not get a tax deduction for the running costs associated with accommodation because the Taxman doesn't accept that this expense is "wholly and exclusively" for the purpose of the company's trade. This would be the case if it wasn't clear that it had been used for business purposes.

37.5.3. High-risk

You only use the accommodation for private purposes and pretend that it is a business asset. Little or no declaration is made for the benefit-in-kind of this private use. You wait six years and hope the Taxman doesn't pick this up before then. If he does, there will be the overdue tax, interest and penalties to pay on the disallowed running costs as well as the value of the benefit-in-kind.

CHAPTER 38

Advisors' fees

38.1. THE EXPENSE

Your company probably receives an annual bill with lots of zeros from advisors for their professional services during the year - such as accounts, tax and consultancy. But in amongst all these there could be costs for time spent on your personal tax affairs. Is this really an issue for the Taxman?

38.2. WHAT IT MIGHT COST

Any personal tax work paid for by the company is treated as a benefit-in-kind and so taxable. As a director, any benefit-in-kind you receive from the company has to be included on your annual return of benefits form (P11D) that the company sends to the Taxman.

If you forget to put this benefit on the P11D, then (if discovered) the company could be liable for a fine of up to £3,000 for filing an incomplete return (although in practice this is rarely levied). But the company will have to pay employers' NI on the benefit omitted at 13.8% of its value.

As you're viewed as receiving a benefit from the company, you have to pay income tax on the value of this at your highest rate of tax.

But how do you put a value on the completion of your tax return and other personal tax work? If it's not specified on your advisor's bill, then the Taxman would estimate the value, either as: **(1)** an estimated percentage of your advisor's overall bill or; **(2)** an estimate of the number of hours that could have been charged by the most expensive advisor in town (plus VAT).

38.3. WHAT ARE THE POTENTIAL TAX SAVINGS?

If you pay your advisor's fees out of your own pocket, then it's likely that this comes out of income that has already suffered tax. If it's income from your company, this money has probably been extracted as either salary or dividends. If you can reduce your tax bill by getting the company to pay direct, then you are in a winning situation.

38.4. THE PAPERWORK

You've reassessed your remuneration package to include personal tax return completion you would like the company to incur, as a benefit-in-kind for yourself. What your company needs to do is put this arrangement in writing - both amongst the company board minutes and as an addition to your contract of employment.

38.4.1. The board minute

If you go down the benefit-in-kind route, your company's board minutes should include a commercial reason for the company agreeing to include your advisor's fees as part of your remuneration package.

EXAMPLE

The board minute covering advisors' fees reads as follows:

"In recognition of your contribution to the company and to avoid the distraction of making sure you have paid the right amount of tax, the company has decided that as part of your remuneration package that it will contract and pay for the advisor's fees for completing and submitting your annual personal tax return. This is, of course, subject to the company having sufficient funds to do so. This does not include any premium for fee protection insurance that the advisor may offer you. This must be paid direct by yourself."

38.4.2. Your contract of employment

Your company needs to put this addition to your remuneration package in writing as an amendment to your contract of employment.

EXAMPLE

Amendment to contract of employment:

"As from November 30 2011, the company will contract and pay for advisor's fees for completion and submission of your annual personal tax return. This benefit-in-kind is from that date part of your remuneration package with the company and will be provided by it subject to the company having sufficient funds to do so."

38.4.3. Contract with/invoice from the supplier

You need the advisor's service to be treated as a benefit-in-kind. As such, the contract with them needs to be negotiated by, addressed to and be clearly a liability of the company (not yours).

TIP

Agree a reasonable cost with your advisor for personal tax services. Then obtain a separate invoice addressed to the company for this nominal amount you have agreed. They will probably do your personal work at "cost" anyway - as a loss leader to the main company account.

38.4.4. On the VAT return

If your company has been charged VAT by the advisor, then it should be able to claim it back via its VAT return.

38.4.5. On your P11D

Your company needs to enter on your P11D the cost to it of providing you with this service from an advisor as a benefit-in-kind (inclusive of VAT) during the tax year.

38.4.6. In the company's accounts

Transfer the cost of this work out of "professional fees" and into "staff costs". This reinforces your company's argument that it is part of your remuneration package and hence it can claim a tax deduction for it.

38.4.7. Your tax return

You simply take the figure given to you by the company for your P11D benefit and put it on your tax return. No further disclosures are required by you.

38.5. LOW, MEDIUM AND HIGH-RISK STRATEGIES

38.5.1. Low-risk

Personal tax services paid for by the company are a taxable benefit. Avoid the Taxman choosing a figure to suit himself by agreeing a nominal figure with your advisor for the work done.

If you get the paperwork right, the low-risk strategy is the one outlined above.

38.5.2. Medium-risk

The company doesn't get a tax deduction for part of your advisor's fees because the Taxman doesn't accept that this expense is "wholly and exclusively" for the purpose of the company's trade. This would be the case if it wasn't clear that the company was paying for, say, your personal tax return to be dealt with as part of your remuneration package.

38.5.3. High-risk

You leave the total fee from your advisor in "professional fees" and don't split out any private element.

If the Taxman actually asks *"who pays for your tax return?"*, can't you just tell him you did it all yourself? Well you could try this approach. But the Taxman may already have authority from you to deal with your advisor direct on your tax affairs. If he has correspondence on file showing that he has done work for you, your argument would look a little weak. What would stick out like a sore thumb would be if your advisor had used a piece of computer software to produce a return which was not available to you. Or if filled in manually, hadn't it better look like your own handwriting?

The real sting in the tail is that the Taxman can go back up to six years to work out how much NI and tax is owed. With interest on top, this could mean the company ends up facing quite a bill.

CHAPTER 39

Parking near work

39.1. THE EXPENSE

The Taxman doesn't allow you to claim the expense of your ordinary commuting to work (including car parking) against your own personal tax. Although you might regard it as necessary in order to be able to turn up for work, he doesn't think it's necessary to do your job. A fine distinction indeed but one he has stuck to and won cases with. However, what if the company pays for the parking instead?

If your company were to apply for and pay for a season ticket for parking at or near to work, you would not be taxed on the cost of this. There's no employers' NI on this payment and the company gets a Corporation Tax deduction. (Even if you've already paid for a parking permit at or near work, you can be reimbursed tax-free.)

But how near is near? The space doesn't have to be provided in a car park immediately adjacent to or attached to the office, but it must be located within a reasonable distance, to be regarded as "at or near work" by the Taxman.

39.2. WHAT IT MIGHT COST

EXAMPLE

Let's say that in your local car park you pay £3.50 a day for 230 days (allowing for bank holidays, annual leave of four weeks and sick leave) that's £805 you are out of pocket. That's equivalent to gross salary or bonus from your company of £1,184 (£805/68%) if you're a basic rate taxpayer; for a higher rate taxpayer it's £1,388 (£805/58%) you'll need to be paid before deduction of tax and NI just to able to afford the parking.

39.3. WHAT ARE THE POTENTIAL TAX SAVINGS?

If you pay for parking near work out of your own pocket, then it's likely that this comes out of income that has already suffered tax. If it's income from your company, this money has probably been extracted as either salary or dividends. If you can reduce your tax bill by getting the company to pay direct, then you are in a winning situation.

Once you get to appreciate the potential tax savings that are to be had you might even agree to take your next pay rise in the form of a parking permit rather than cash.

EXAMPLE

Penny earns £21,500 a year and currently pays £3.50 a day to park her car near the office. This costs her £805 a year out of her taxed income. If Penny forgoes a 4% pay increase (£21,500 x 4% = £645) in return for free parking which costs the company £645 (with a discount for a paying in advance) on an annual season ticket, the savings are as follows:

	£	£
Cost saved on parking		805.00
4% pay rise sacrificed (*)	645.00	
Tax at 20% on £645	(129.00)	
NI at 12% £645	(77.40)	
Net pay forgone		438.00
Net saving		366.40

(*) The employer saves NI at 13.8% on the cost of the season ticket instead of paying salary.

39.4.   THE PAPERWORK

39.4.1. Parking permit

Get your company to apply and pay for a season ticket for parking at or near to work, and you will not be taxed on the cost of this.

39.4.2. Salary sacrifice

Any agreement to replace salary or a pay rise with a free parking permit must be made in advance of the pay rise taking effect on that salary. If substitution is made in arrears, the Taxman will ignore the reduction in the cash salary and continue to tax the original gross salary amount.

39.4.3. On your P11D

Your company doesn't need to enter anything on your P11D.

39.4.4. In the company's accounts

Leave the cost of this parking within, say, "motor expenses".

39.4.5. Your tax return

There is nothing for you to enter on your personal tax return.

39.5. LOW, MEDIUM AND HIGH-RISK STRATEGIES

39.5.1. Low-risk

If your company pays in advance for parking at or near your workplace, the cost of this is free of tax and NI (for both of you). Indeed, taken as a substitute for salary this could save both even more tax. Of course you need to get the paperwork right up-front.

39.5.2. Medium-risk

Any agreement to replace salary or a pay rise with a free parking permit must be made in advance of the pay rise taking effect on that salary. If substitution is made in arrears, the Taxman will ignore the reduction in the cash salary and continue to tax the original gross salary amount.

39.5.3. High-risk

The parking near work turns out to be parking somewhere else, e.g. for a railway station car park or even near your flat in town! The real sting in the tail here is that the Taxman can go back up to six years to work out how much NI and tax is owed. With interest on top, this could mean the company ends up facing quite a bill for this misinterpretation of the rules.

CHAPTER 40

Computer equipment

40.1. THE EXPENSE

Computer equipment plays such an important part of modern life that it's not just confined to the workplace. Whether it's for gaming, the children's schoolwork or communicating with friends or family on the other side of the world, the majority of households now possess at least one computer. But with technological change becoming increasingly rapid, maintaining up-to-date systems can be difficult and expensive. It would be nice to let your company foot the bill.

Things were fine until April 5 2006 because an employer was able to lend a computer to an employee for entirely private use at home and there was no taxable benefit - provided the computer cost no more than £2,500 or, if it was leased, the rental was no more than £500 a year. In fact, if you're still using this equipment the exemption still applies. However, any computer equipment provided to you by your company from April 6 2006 for private use is now chargeable to tax as a benefit-in-kind each year.

Memory sticks

Computer users have long complained that for backing up files, 3-inch floppy disks are too unstable, the ZIP drive not practical and CDs not portable enough. One of the answers to these complaints is the memory stick, which is small, portable and a very stable data storage device. Ideal for quickly backing up and restoring company computer files in the office or at home.

In future get the company to buy the memory sticks and then hand them out. If your company has a policy of writing off all fixed assets under, say £100, then there's no need to add this hardware to the fixed asset record in your accounts. They can be written off straight to computer expenses in your profit and loss account to get an immediate tax deduction for the company.

40.2. WHAT IT MIGHT COST

The benefit-in-kind for the company lending you a computer for private use is measured as 20% of its market value when first provided or the lease rental charge if higher. Remember, companies pay 13.8% Class 1A NI on benefits-in-kind.

EXAMPLE

The computer you've got at home is fast becoming obsolete and you decide to upgrade it with some new equipment. The system you really want, with all the peripherals, comes to £1,500. Tax on benefit of £300 (£1,500 x 20%) at 40% income tax = £120. Employers' NI on benefits £300 x 13.8% = £41.

However, the company is able to claim back the VAT whereas you aren't. VAT reclaim £1,500 x 20/120 = £250.

EXAMPLE

Spending £39.99 on a 16GB memory stick and claiming it through your tax return as an expense of employment would save you income tax of £8.00 (at 20%) or £16 (at 40%). However, you are still out of pocket by some £31 or £24 respectively. If you've already personally bought a memory stick (and still have the receipt), then charge this to your company to get your full cost back. This is more tax efficient than trying to claim it back through your own tax return.

40.3. WHAT ARE THE POTENTIAL TAX SAVINGS?

If you pay for the IT equipment yourself, it will come from income that's already had tax deducted from it. However, if the company pays then you save some of the tax that you would have paid on that income withdrawal. The potential savings are examined below.

40.3.1. Savings on your salary

If the company pays for your IT equipment, the payments will be taxed under the benefit-in-kind rules on you as the director/employee of the company. Computer equipment is chargeable to tax as a benefit-in-kind each year, measured as 20% of the market value of the computer when first provided or the lease rental charge if higher. Employers pay 13.8% Class 1A NI on benefits-in-kind.

The tax on this benefit will be less than the tax you would have normally paid under PAYE to get the same net amount of income to make the purchase yourself. In addition, there won't be any employees' NI to pay. The company will have an NI bill to pay, but once again it will be on a lesser amount than the salary equivalent.

EXAMPLE

Your company buys a computer package costing £1,500 (including VAT). It lends it to you to use at home for personal computing. How is this cheaper tax wise than buying it yourself?

40.3.2. You

	40% TAXPAYER (£)
Tax on salary £1,500 (42/58)	1,086
Tax on £1,500 dividend	37
Tax on benefit of £300 (£1,500 x 20%)	120

For a 40% taxpayer the highest tax saving comes from taking a benefit-in-kind.

40.3.3. Your company and NI

	40% TAXPAYER (£)
NI on salary @ 13.8% on £2,586	357
NI on dividend	-
NI on benefits £300 @ 13.8%	41

40.3.4. VAT

The company is able to claim back the VAT whereas you aren't. The VAT reclaim in this example is worth £1,500 x 20/120 = £250.

40.4. THE PAPERWORK

By taking the following steps you will be making sure that there is no room for a challenge by the Taxman. And with all the paperwork done correctly there should be no risk of penalties arising at a later date either.

40.4.1. The board minute

Remember, any expense charged in the company's accounts has to meet the "wholly and exclusively" test that we talked about earlier. Getting a formal board minute drawn up demonstrates to the Taxman that the benefit was agreed on by the company as a way of rewarding you for your services to the company. There is no need for any special wording, just a statement of the facts as a record for future reference.

EXAMPLE

"Meeting of the Board of Directors of XYZ Limited on .... at ....

It was resolved that the company approve the purchase of IT equipment for .... to the value of .... (insert figure) as part of their remuneration package.

This award has been made in recognition of their continuing contribution to the success of the company.

Signed .... company secretary."

40.4.2. Contract of employment

Because this is a variation of your remuneration package you will need to incorporate it into your contract of employment by way of an addendum.

EXAMPLE

"As of .... the company will pay for new IT equipment to the value of .... (insert figure) for your own personal use. This benefit-in-kind is to be treated as part of your remuneration package with the company."

40.4.3. Contract with/invoice from the supplier

Getting the supplier to invoice the company will make it absolutely clear that the liability for payment belongs with the company and not you.

40.4.4. On the VAT return

As the contract is with the company, any VAT charged on the purchase of the computer equipment can be reclaimed on your company's VAT return.

40.4.5. On your P11D

The value of the benefit-in-kind to be included is 20% of the total cost of the equipment before the deduction of VAT.

40.4.6. In the company's accounts

There are no special disclosure requirements, the IT equipment gets lost in the fixed asset additions total shown in the accounts.

40.4.7. On your tax return

Simply transfer the values from your P11D to the relevant boxes on your tax return's employment pages. Any tax due will then be collected in the normal way.

40.5. LOW, MEDIUM AND HIGH-RISK STRATEGIES

40.5.1. Low-risk

Getting the paperwork right as described above cuts all risk down to an absolute minimum.

Buy memory sticks for your employees (including yourself) for back-up purposes. This is more tax efficient than an employee buying the storage and then trying to claim it back for tax.

40.5.2. Medium-risk

If it's unclear that the payment is part of your remuneration package, there's a risk that the company won't be allowed a deduction in the accounts under the "true and fair" rules. This means a loss of Corporation Tax relief.

40.5.3. High-risk

A high-risk strategy here would be for the company to pay for the equipment without declaring anything to the Taxman about its private use. You will get away with paying no tax on the benefits and having the tax relief on the purchase. However, if discovered, the Taxman will hit the company with a bill for the tax and NI unpaid. In addition, there will be the fines for incorrect P11Ds and interest for late payment of tax due.

Technical notes

In Section 1 of this book we set out the ground rules for legitimately putting expenses through your business. In Section 2 you can see how much more of your money you'll be able to keep for yourself and away from the Taxman's grasp. Never forget that the Taxman only ever gives you his biased interpretation of what is allowed. Hence these notes which supplement Section 2. They incorporate references to statutory and other authorities, and the abbreviations used are those conventionally adopted by taxation advisors.

For example, the **Income Tax (Employment and Pensions) Act** is abbreviated to "ITEPA" and the **Taxman's Employment Income Manual** to "EIM".

References to "the Taxman" is our shorthand for HM Revenue & Customs (HMRC). And a reference to married couples includes same-sex couples who have registered under the **Civil Partnership Act 2004**.

Our references to paragraphs in the Taxman's own manuals can be followed up by visiting http://www.hmrc.gov.uk/manuals/.

21.   USE OF HOME BY A COMPANY

The £3 per week

When an employee works at home for some or all of the time, he or she may incur additional household costs, for example in heating and lighting. The employer may make payments to the employee tax-free and without any liability for NI contributions (NICs) to help to meet those additional costs.

The employer can pay up to £3 per week (£156 per year) without obtaining any supporting evidence of the additional costs **(s.316A ITEPA 2003)**. The employer can pay more than that where evidence is retained to show that the amount paid is no greater than the additional costs incurred by the employee.

Scale rate payments **EIM05200** that reimburse the average expenses met by employees working at home can be paid tax-free and without any liability for NICs if the amount has been agreed by a tax inspector.

Tax Bulletin 79 http://www.hmrc.gov.uk/bulletins/tb79.htm#a "Employees Who Work At Home - Tax Relief For Unreimbursed Homeworking Expenses - **s.336 ITEPA 2003**".

There is a new page in **EIM01471** for employees who work from home. It distinguishes between the situation where: **(1)** the employer pays expenses under a homeworking arrangement **(s.316A ITEPA)**; and **(2)** the employer doesn't pay so the employee must claim on their own tax return **(s.366 ITEPA)**.

Rent

Where an employer claims that the payment to an employee is rent chargeable on the employee as property income, then this is tax deductible for the company and not earnings of the employee **(EIM01400)**.

22. GARDEN MAINTENANCE

In order to manage the business a company has to attract and retain key employees. The cost of this usually meets the "wholly and exclusively" test, provided it's not excessive for the duties performed. Therefore, if you reassess your remuneration package (as an employee) to include in it, say, garden maintenance that you want your company to incur (as a benefit-in-kind for yourself) this is, in our opinion, "wholly and exclusively for the purposes of the trade" too. However, if challenged on this "part of your remuneration" argument by the Taxman, you'll need to be able to provide him with a copy of what was agreed in writing.

National Minimum Wage (NMW)

The remuneration defence against a "wholly and exclusively" attack relies on you actually having a contract of employment with your company. According to the Department for Business Enterprise and Regulatory Reform guidance, the NMW will apply to directors if they have a contract of employment, as this makes them workers.

23. GIFTS

Gifts not taxable as earnings

A gift does **not** count as earnings within **s.62 ITEPA 2003** if it is made:

- on personal grounds (for example, a wedding present); or
- as a mark of personal esteem or appreciation.

(EIM01460)

If the gift is a genuine one - that is, a personal and unexpected gift made from an employer to an employee, given as a gesture of goodwill or as a token of gratitude - the payment is not earnings and, therefore, no NI is due **(NIM02165)**.

Trivial benefits

You can ask for a benefit to be exempt from tax on the grounds that the cash equivalent of the benefit taxable on the employee is so trivial as to be not worth pursuing **(EIM21860)**. Examples of trivial benefits can be found at **EIM21863**.

Annual parties and other social functions

Directors and employees are chargeable on their share of the expense incurred by an employer in providing a social function for employees, except where **s.264 ITEPA 2003** exempts the charge to tax **(EIM21690)**. Examples can be found at **EIM21691**. The exemption applies to an annual party (for example, a Christmas party), or similar annual function (for example, a summer barbecue), provided for employees and is:

- available to employees generally; or
- available to employees generally at one location, where the employer has more than one location.

There can be more than one annual function, as long as the total for all functions per head does not exceed £150, then all are tax-free.

Note. In practice (if they spot it) local inspectors have been known to argue that this expense is not for the purpose of the business in husband and wife companies and thus not give a Corporation Tax deduction or try to assess the amounts as taxable. This is on the basis that you will think it costs too much to challenge him and so will back down. If he would allow it for larger companies ask him why he is discriminating against your company.

24. LANGUAGE LESSONS

Your company can get a full tax deduction for any work-related training it provides to its employees, which includes you as a director **(s.250 ITEPA 2003)**. The company must contract and pay for the training directly. The employee is not allowed tax relief for the cost of training paid personally. Case: **Consultant Psychiatrist v Revenue & Customs 2006 STC 653**. "Work-related" means any skill the employee may have need of at work either now or in the future, or even when the employee works in a voluntary capacity on behalf of the firm, such as helping a local charity.

See also **EIM01210**.

25. MAGAZINE SUBSCRIPTIONS

EIM32880 - professional fees and subscriptions.

s.343 and s.344 ITEPA 2003.

If the body is not on "List 3" (http://www.hmrc.gov.uk/list3/list3.pdf) you won't get a tax deduction for the subscription.

26. PAYING FOR A HOLIDAY

A benefit provided for a member of an employee's family or household, whether by their employer or someone else, is chargeable on them under the benefits code if it is provided by reason of their employment. If the benefit is provided by the employee's employer it is deemed to be provided by reason of the employment **(s.201(3) ITEPA 2003 and EIM20502)**.

"Family or household" **(s.721(4) ITEPA 2003)** means:

- the employee's spouse or civil partner
- the employee's children and their spouses or civil partners
- the employee's parents
- the employee's dependants
- the employee's domestic staff
- the employee's guests (that is people staying at their invitation in their home or in accommodation provided by them).

Thus an employee who takes their family away on holiday at their employer's expense is chargeable not only on the cost of their own holiday fares and accommodation but also on the cost of those relating to their spouse and family.

27. PRIVATE TUTORS

Before April 6 2005 childcare vouchers couldn't be used to pay for any form of education, but the law now says that the qualifying care can be any form of care or supervised activity that is not part of the child's compulsory education **(s.318B(1) ITEPA 2003)**. So as long as the subject of your child's extra lessons is not covered in compulsory school hours, in their particular school, it can be paid for directly by your company or with childcare vouchers up to the tax-free limit.

The second condition for the childcare to be tax and NI-free, is that it must be provided by a registered or approved childcarer.

28. SCHOOL FEES

The trick is to get the educational establishment to agree to contract directly with your company so that the company is liable to pay the fees in all circumstances. In this case, you can avoid paying employees' NI - a saving of up to 12% of the cost of the fees.

In the case of **Frost Skip Hire (Newcastle) Ltd v IRC SpC (2004)**, the company had agreed with the school to pay the fees of the director's son. Invoices for fees due were rendered to the company, which paid them. However, it was the parents, not the company, who signed the original school entry forms that contained terms and conditions making them personally liable for the fees. There was no evidence of any renegotiation of contracts between the company and the school. So it was deemed that the company was meeting a liability of the parents and both employers' and employees' NI was due on the total fees paid.

Even if you get all the paperwork right so the contract is genuinely between the school/university and the company, you will still be taxed on the fees paid as a benefit-in-kind. The company is paying the school fees because you are its employee. This was shown in the case **Glyn v CIR (Hong Kong) 1990**. The company had agreed in the taxpayer's contract of employment to pay his child's boarding school fees while he worked in Hong Kong. The school fees were held to be part of the taxpayer's total remuneration package and were taxable as a benefit-in-kind. This is as long as you can justify the level of remuneration for work done.

See   http://www.hmrc.gov.uk/paye/exb/a-z/s/school-fees.htm   the   Taxman's summary for this expense.

29.   PERSONAL TRAINER

To obtain a tax deduction in the company, your argument is that the contract with the personal trainer is within "the benefits code" and hence is part of your employment income. This is best taken care of by adding the provision by the company of a personal trainer to your contract of employment.

Payment of bills. Liability will depend upon who enters into the contract with the party supplying the goods or services. The address on the bill does not have any bearing on who contracted for the supply/provision of the goods or services **(NIM02270)**.

30.   CARS FOR THE FAMILY

Members of your family or household are defined at **EIM20504** and **s.721 (4) ITEPA 2003**.

31. COMPANY PLANE (OR YACHT)

Aeroplane

For the Taxman's valuation (including VAT) of the benefit-in-kind for private use of a company aeroplane, see the example at **EIM21638**.

EIM21637 - mixed (private v business) use assets placed at the disposal of a director or employee.

CA27300 - assets used partly for a qualifying activity.

Yacht

For the Taxman's valuation of the benefit-in-kind for private use of a company yacht, see the example at **EIM21633** and **s.205 ITEPA 2003**.

32. GYM MEMBERSHIP

An employer can pay a club membership fee for directors or employees. The expense incurred will be a benefit chargeable on directors and employees **(EIM21696)**. If you pay a composite subscription entitling all employees to membership, liability arises on directors and employees who are not lower paid (more than £8,500 p.a. including the value of any benefits). Any reasonable apportionment of the total subscription cost amongst employees should be accepted **(EIM01060)**.

Club membership is mainly a personal and social matter, giving rise to amenities and privileges limited to members. Any suggestion that the cost of membership of a club is deductible as a necessary expense incurred in the performance of the duties of the employment would normally be rejected by the Taxman **(EIM32500)**. Therefore, to obtain a tax deduction in the company your argument is that the membership fee is paid by an employer for a director or employee within "the benefits code" as part of your contract of employment.

The exemption route

No charge on earnings as employment income arises from the provision by employers for employees, former employees or members of their families or households of:

- qualifying sports or recreational facilities **(s.261(2) ITEPA 2003)**; or
- non-cash vouchers exchangeable only for the use of such facilities

- A qualifying sports or recreational benefit or facility is one that:

  - is available generally to all the employees of the employer concerned **(s.261(3)**
  - facilities provided for a few, selected employees only do not qualify); and

- is not available to members of the public generally **(s.261(4))**

- is used wholly or mainly by employees or former employees and members of their families or household **(s.261(5)) (EIM21825)**.

If the company premises are not also domestic premises, it can pay for a fitness instructor to take classes there for the benefit of all the workers (although not everyone may join in). Similarly, the company can provide fitness equipment to be used at the company's premises, which must also not be domestic premises.

33.　GARAGE STORAGE

Any allowance paid to you for use of your garage by your company counts as earnings. Therefore, PAYE should be applied to the payment. This will be the case whether or not the garage is attached to your home **(s.62 ITEPA 2003 and EIM01400)**.

Where an employer claims that the payment to an employee is rent chargeable on the employee as property income, then this is tax deductible for the company and not earnings of the employee **(EIM01400)**. There must be a lease in place between the employee and the company.

Case law: **Beecham Group v Fair (1983)** - where PAYE needs to be applied.

Strictly, the employee should be paying rent to a third party for use of a garage, for the reimbursement from their company to be tax-free.

34.　NANNIES

Liability will depend upon who enters into the contract with the party supplying the goods or services. The address on the bill does not have any bearing on who contracted for the supply/provision of the goods or services **(NIM02270)**.

Childcare vouchers can be used to pay for nannies who work in the home, if the nanny is "approved" under the childcare approval scheme in England. The nanny must pay tax on the value of the childcare voucher as it is part of their remuneration, see: http://www.hmrc.gov.uk/childcare/questions-and-answering.htm.

35. THE WEEKEND AWAY

s.337 to **s.339 ITEPA 2003.**

EIM31811 - expenses do not have to be "wholly and exclusively" incurred: example.

EIM31815 - associated subsistence.

EIM31820 and EIM02710 - other incidental costs/expenses.

EIM31950 - overseas conferences, seminars and study tours.

36. DOMESTIC HELP

An employer may provide domestic help, in the form of paying for chefs, cleaners etc.

s.62 ITEPA 2003.

Booklet 480(2011) Expenses and benefits A tax guide. Types of taxable benefit "work carried out at the employee's residence" http://www.hmrc.gov.uk/guidance/480.pdf.

The domestic help needs to be genuinely self-employed to avoid the risk of these payments later being classed made to "employees" of the company, with additional tax and NI bills.

Paying bills. Liability will depend upon who enters into the contract with the party supplying the goods or services. The address on the bill does not have any bearing on who contracted for the supply/provision of the goods or services **(NIM02270)**.

If for a more remote relative, e.g. mother-in-law not living in the same household, then possibly no taxable benefit arises. Of course, the company won't get a deduction for the remote relative's cleaner as they are not for the purpose of the business.

37. USE OF THE COMPANY VILLA

Living accommodation: meaning of provided

The cash equivalent value of the benefit from living accommodation that is "provided" for an employee is taxable. The meaning of provided is often an issue in the case of holiday accommodation. It is not defined in the legislation and its meaning has not been considered by the courts in this context. So the word is given its ordinary dictionary meaning by the Taxman: supplied or furnished with a thing. In some cases provided will mean available for use, whereas in others it will mean actually used.

In deciding whether "provided" means available for use, or means actually used, the following questions will be asked by the Taxman **(EIM11406)**:

- who can use the living accommodation? The Taxman accepts that if living accommodation is genuinely available for use by more people than could actually use it at any one time, then provided only means the periods actually used. For example if five unrelated employees were allowed to use an employer owned two bedroom holiday villa we would only seek a provided living accommodation charge on each employee for the period in which that employee actually used the villa

- why was the living accommodation bought or rented and how has it been used since acquisition? If the living accommodation was bought as holiday accommodation for a director and family, provided is likely to mean available for use. By contrast, if it was bought as a genuine letting business by the employer and has been let out commercially, then provided will only mean the periods of actual use by the employee.

For examples illustrating these points see **EIM11421**.

Finance Act 2008 introduced an exemption **(s.100A ITEPA 2003)** to prevent a benefit-in-kind arising where overseas holiday homes are held through a non-trading company, and the only purpose of that company is to hold property. (**NIM11371** onwards).

38. ADVISORS' FEES

No special legislation relating to these fees. The charge to tax is therefore under either **s.62 ITEPA 2003** or under the benefits code.

Case law: **Pepper v Hart (1992)**.

EIM13740 - legal fees regarding termination of employment.

39. PARKING NEAR WORK

There is no tax charge **(s.237 ITEPA 2003)** on a director or employee within the benefits code on the provision of a car, van or motorcycle parking space at or near (a reasonable distance from) their place of work **(EIM01030)**. Facilities for parking bicycles are also exempt **(EIM21685)**.

40.   COMPUTER EQUIPMENT

Annual value

EIM21632 - 20% of annual value.

When an employee is provided with a benefit by the transfer of the ownership of an asset, the cost of the benefit (this is called the "cash equivalent") is normally the expense incurred by the person providing the benefit, less any amount made good by the employee. If an employee earning at a rate of £8,500 a year or more has an asset placed at their disposal, without any transfer of ownership, there are special rules for the amount of the benefit charge. The cash equivalent is equal to 20% of the market value of the computer when it was first supplied to the employee plus any running costs met by the employer in the year.

The market value of an asset at a particular time is defined **(s.208 ITEPA 2003)** as the price that it might reasonably have been expected to fetch on a sale in the open market at that time.

There is no tax charge on the use of any computer where the private use is not significant **(s.316 ITEPA 2003)**.

Appendices

EXPENSES CLAIM FORM

Expense claim reference: ....

Employee's name: ....

Department: ....

Note. All claims must be supported by a VAT receipt / invoice.

Date	Description	Fares & travel (£)	Subsistence (£)	Mileage (complete separate claim form)	Hotel & accommodation (£)	Postage (£)	Stationery (£)	Entertaining (£)	Other (£)	Total inc. VAT
Total										

I certify that the above expenditure has been necessarily incurred on the Company's business as shown above.

Signed by: ....   Authorised by: ....

Date: ....

Appendices

MILEAGE RECORD

Employee's name: .... Month/year: ....

Make of vehicle: .... Model: .... Engine size (cc): .... Fuel type: ....

Date	To	From	Reason	Miles	Claim (£)
Business mileage brought forward for tax year to date					
Total amount claimed					
Business mileage carried forward for tax year to date					

Notes

1. Use the business mileage b/fwd where you make monthly claims to ensure you do not exceed 10,000 miles per annum limit.

2. Where business mileage is less than 10,000 miles per annum, the claim is up to 45p per mile.

3. Where business mileage exceeds 10,000 miles per annum, the claim is 25p per mile.

4. You should record all travel that is undertaken for business purposes giving as much detail as possible to support your claim.

SAMPLE DISPENSATION COVERING LETTER

Your address: ....

....

....

Date: ....

Dear Taxpayer

I have approved your application and enclose a Dispensation Notice.

The dispensation is effective from April 6 2011. This means from that, from that date, there is no need for the company to enter details of expenses and benefits of the type shown on the Forms P11D.

The notice replaces any earlier dispensation notice issued to you with immediate effect.

This dispensation only applies to expenses and benefits paid in the circumstances prescribed in the enclosed notice. All other expenses and benefits must be reported on Forms P11D.

Please let us know if any of the circumstances change around the expenses payments and benefits. If they do, we will need to check whether the dispensation will continue.

Yours sincerely

Specialist EC Officer

Enc

SAMPLE DISPENSATION NOTICE

[Local Compliance] [Specialist Employer Compliance]

Address: ....

....

....

Date: ....

Our reference: ....

Your reference: ....

Dear Taxpayer

Dispensation for particular expenses payments and other matters

This dispensation applies to the expenses payments, benefits and facilities that are set out below. For the purposes of this dispensation these matters are referred collectively as "expenses payments and benefits". It means you will not have to report these expense payments and benefits at the end of the year on Forms P11D or P9D. It revokes from the date of this dispensation any previous dispensation covering expenses or benefits.

I am giving you this dispensation because I am satisfied, on the basis of what you have told me, that no additional tax would be payable by the employee concerned on these expenses payments and benefits. I am authorised to do this by Section 65 and Section 96 of the Income Tax (Earnings and Pensions) Act 2003.

This dispensation only applies to the expense payments and benefits, set out below, in the circumstances there set out. If the expense payments or benefits are paid or provided in circumstances that give rise to additional tax, this dispensation will need to be revoked. Where necessary, the revocation may apply to expenses or benefits already provided. In that case additional tax and NI will be due.

It is important that you let me know if you alter your system for controlling expense payments and benefits, or increase their amounts, or change their nature or make any other change that might affect their taxability.

Payments and benefits that are in any way different, or are provided in circumstances that differ from those set out below will not be covered by this dispensation and should be reported in the normal way.

Yours sincerely

Authorised Officer of HMRC

Employees covered by this dispensation:

A   Directors, where the directors' expense claims are independently checked by an authorised person, or where full receipts or relevant vouchers are held in support of the expenditure.

B   All other employees whose claims are independently checked and authorised by another person, except

- where the exemptions provided by this dispensation notice and any way would bring their total earnings below £8,500 and

- there are other payments of expenses and benefits which would thereby cease to be taxable under the benefits code Section 63 ITEPA 2003.

Employees not covered by this dispensation:

- non-UK domiciled individuals working in the UK who have an employment relationship with an employer resident outside the UK.

Nature of payments and benefits

1. Entertaining

The cost of entertaining customers or potential customers or potential customers, suppliers or other business connections at genuine business occasions. This section only applies to expenditure that falls to be disallowed in the employer's accounts in accordance with Section 45 ITTOIA 2005 or Section 577 ICTA 1988.

The following can usually be regarded as reasonable and genuine business occasions:

- product launches

- lunches and similar events for customers or potential customers at which business is discussed

- exhibitions and similar events at which products are on display for customers.

Claims for entertaining expenses should be supported with records of the amounts spent on particular occasions, the nature of the entertainment, the persons entertained and the reasons for the entertainment.

2. Professional fees and subscriptions

Professional fees and subscriptions paid by or on behalf of an employee to an organisation, included in HMRC List 3, where the activities of the organisation are relevant to the office of employment in accordance with Section 343 and 344 Income Tax (Earnings and Pensions Act) 2003.

The activities of the organisation are relevant to the office or employment if the performance of the duties is directly affected by the knowledge that the organisation exists to provide, or they involve the exercise of the profession that organisation represents.

3. Home telephone (main line)/personal mobile telephone

Reimbursement of the cost of business calls made from a private home telephone or employee's personal mobile telephone, where justified by reference to the itemised bills. The line rental remains the personal liability of the subscriber.

4. Travel (excluding mileage allowances)

Reimbursement of the costs actually incurred by employees, when supported by receipts, on journeys undertaken for business purposes by road (excluding mileage allowances), rail, air and sea, but excluding ordinary commuting.

Minor business travel expenditure such as parking, road and bridge tolls and tube fares for which receipts are not available may be reimbursed under the terms of this dispensation notice providing that there is an alternative supporting documentation to confirm that the expenses were necessarily incurred.

For further guidance on qualifying business travel please see Booklet 490 (Employee Travel - A tax and NICs guide for employers).

Exclusion of ordinary commuting. Travel between an employees' home, or any other place that is not a workplace, and his/her normal place of work is ordinary commuting and is not covered by the dispensation.

Note. Dispensations are no longer available in respect of mileage allowances paid to employees using their own vehicles for business travel. Amounts not exceeding the qualifying amount, the number of miles of business travel multiplied by the currently applicable rates, are exempt from tax. Amounts in excess of the approved amount are always taxable. The current rates can be found at http://www.hmrc.gov.uk/rates/travel.htm. Earlier rates can be found from a link on that page.

5. Subsistence

The reasonable and necessary cost of a meal/snack and beverages incurred by an employee whilst undertaking the expenses of which are included in the section relating to Travel (excluding mileage allowances). The travel must occupy the whole or a substantial part of a working day encompassing the normal meal breaks. Claims must be supported by relevant receipts.

The reasonable cost when supported the relevant receipts or invoices of accommodation, breakfast, lunch, if applicable, and an evening meal (except were accompanied by a spouse or relative etc.) incurred by an employee who is required to stay overnight in the course of such a journey. The travel can be either within or outside the UK but the employee must be working away on company business.

Excluded from the dispensation are the cost of videos, newspapers, beverages not complementing an evening meal and private telephone calls, all of which are covered by the legislation relating to incidental overnight expenses. (Please read Appendix 8 of the HMRC booklet 480 for further information).

The maximum amounts of incidental overnight expenses that an employer may reimburse free of tax are £5 per night for overnight stays anywhere within the UK (GB and NI) and £10 per night for stays outside the UK.

If the total amount paid exceeds the maximum tax-free amount for the period of absence, the whole of the payment becomes taxable not just the excess.

6. Company credit cards

This dispensation covers goods or services obtained by means of a company credit/debit card supplied by reason of employment. The employee must reimburse the employer in full for any personal expenses incurred. The cost of any business-related goods or services obtained by the use of the credit card must be in such circumstances that, had the employee incurred it, there would be a deduction for it under Sections 336-338 of the Income Tax (Earnings and Pensions) Act 2003.

Enc

EXPENSES POLICY

1. General principles

The principle of the Expenses Policy is to ensure that staff continue to be reimbursed for all necessary expenditure reasonably incurred in the performance of their Company duties. The basis of expense claims will be actual expenditure up to limits as specified in this Policy; limits will be reviewed annually. Staff must pay for their personal expenses and claim them back; invoicing the Company direct should only be used to settle the cost of group events (excluding entertaining) which exceed £ ………. *(insert figure)*.

Managers and staff should note that authorising managers have no authority to vary this Policy; claims for items not allowed under the policy will be rejected. Staff should note that if they pay for expenses incurred by another individual, any deductions from their claim for non-compliance with this policy would be their responsibility.

Failure to comply with this policy may be treated as a disciplinary matter.

2. Guidelines on how to claim your expenses

Timeliness of submission

Expenses should be submitted as soon as possible after they have been incurred. However, it costs a certain amount to process any claim, so claimants should endeavour not to submit claims for less than £ …………. *(insert figure)*, unless they represent the total of expenses in a three-month period. A claim that is more than three months old will only be paid in exceptional circumstances and will require second level authorisation.

Receipts

Original receipts must accompany all claims. Credit card slips or statements will not be accepted as evidence of business expenditure. A VAT receipt must include the name and address of the retailer, the retailer's VAT registration number, the date of the purchase, details of what goods or services have been purchased and the VAT inclusive value of those goods or services in sterling. A VAT registration number consists of nine digits.

3. Authorisation of expenses

All expense claims must be authorised by a more senior manager who is familiar with your work schedule and did not attend any event being claimed for. Authorising managers must ensure they are happy with the claim, or reject it for correction or further information. Certain claims or items may require additional authorisation by the Finance Director.

4. Mileage

When driving on Company business, provided it is further from your home to your temporary destination than it is from your home to your normal place of work, you can claim the lower of the distance: **(1)** from your home to your temporary destination; or **(2)** from your normal place of work to the temporary destination.

Driving a private vehicle

Mileage should normally be claimed at the official HMRC approved rates below, which apply regardless of engine size:

Miles per tax year	Car	Motorcycle	Bicycle
Up to 10,000 miles	45p	24p	20p
Over 10,000 miles	25p	24p	20p

Although there is no direct relationship between fuel purchases and business mileage, where possible please submit a VAT fuel receipt with your claim in order to allow the Company to recover VAT on mileage.

Driving a Company car

If you have a Company car for business use, or you receive cash or pension instead of a car, you will only be able to reclaim the mileage costs at the rates below (from March 1 2011):

	Up to 1,400cc	1,401 - 2,000cc	Over 2,000cc
Petrol	14p	16p	23p
Diesel	13p	13p	16p
LPG	10p	12p	17p

5. Miscellaneous driving expenses

Parking. Reasonable car parking costs while on business will be met.

Tolls and congestion charges. Necessary road and bridge toll costs will be met, including the congestion charge where there is a genuine business need to incur it. No tolls or congestion charges can be claimed for travel between home and work.

Fines. Fines for any motoring offences, including parking tickets, incurred by drivers whilst using a vehicle must be paid promptly by the individual. Failure to do so will result in the cost of the fine and administration fee being recovered directly from the driver. In exceptional cases an authorising manager may agree to reimburse a fine incurred as a result of an emergency and this should be recovered via expenses; any such reimbursement may give rise to a tax liability which will be met by the Company.

Driving a hire car. Vehicles should only be rented for business purposes where it is cost effective and when public transportation and minicabs are impractical, more expensive or not available. Where a traveller has a vehicle which has been supplied by the Company a vehicle must not be rented unless the Company vehicle is off the road due to an accident. The class of vehicle booked should be the minimum size and specification necessary to allow duties to be performed. Bookings should be made through the Company's preferred supplier(s).

Staff who are eligible for a company car, but who receive cash or pension instead of a car, are not entitled to hire a car at the Company's cost.

Authorised drivers. The only persons authorised to drive hire cars are Company employees, or properly contracted freelancers, who have completed (and had authorised) a driver declaration form.

Fuel. The cost of fuel used on business can be reimbursed by submitting an appropriate receipt. Vehicles should be returned with a full tank.

Insurance. Company insurance provides third party insurance and collision damage waiver in respect of vehicles registered in the UK and Ireland. This only covers Company business use by an authorised driver. Any personal use of the vehicle by an authorised driver is not covered. Depending on the circumstances the cost of damage to a hired vehicle may be recovered from the driver.

For vehicles hired outside of these countries, insurance cover is provided by the car rental supplier as part of the Company business rates and will be subject to local terms and conditions. Personal accident and emergency medical insurance is not included in these rates.

6. Overseas expenses

The principles of the rest of this Policy continue to apply when travelling overseas on Company business. This section highlights the differences permitted overseas.

Overnight accommodation. The basis of claims is actuality. The level of expenditure should be appropriate to the country visited but with the aim of staying within the UK rate if possible. Any claims for accommodation costing more than £ .... *(insert figure)* (excluding VAT) a night must be justified and will require second level authorisation.

Meals. The basis of claims is actuality. The level of expenditure should be appropriate to the country visited and for most countries this is unlikely to exceed the UK limits below, which include local taxes and service:

Meal	Limit (incl. VAT and service)
Breakfast	£5
Lunch	£5
Dinner	£10

Incidental expenses. The actual cost of incidental expenses, such as personal telephone calls, newspapers, laundry (normally after seven nights away), any necessary medication (such as malaria tablets) and bottled water may be claimed where appropriate. (**Note.** If the total reimbursed for such incidental overnight expenses exceeds £10 a night, the total will be a taxable benefit).

Passport and visa requirements. It is the traveller's responsibility to maintain a current passport with more than six months until the expiry date and to ensure that any visas which are required are obtained in advance of travel. Cost of visas can be recovered. Frequent travellers may claim for the cost of a second passport.

Health and safety. Travellers are responsible for checking, implementing and maintaining on an ongoing basis any necessary health requirements for the destinations to which they are travelling. Appropriate health advice is available from the Foreign Office/WHO. The cost of inoculations can be reclaimed on production of a receipt and a copy of the relevant Foreign Office/WHO advice.

Hiring a vehicle. Vehicles should only be rented overseas for business purposes where it is cost effective and when public transportation and minicabs are impractical, more expensive or not available. The class of vehicle booked should be the minimum size and specification necessary to allow duties to be performed. Bookings should be made through the Company's preferred supplier(s).

Exchange rates. Foreign currency transactions should preferably be claimed at the actual exchange rate incurred. Where the Company's default exchange rate is used, an additional claim may be made for any material difference between the default rate and the rate actually incurred, on production of a copy of the bank or credit card statement.

7. Personal travel and incentives

Personal travel linked to Company business. Personal travel as part of a business trip is discouraged, and in any event only allowed where such travel actually reduces the cost of business travel to the Company, e.g. staying a Saturday night to take advantage of a lower cost airfare. Where additional costs are incurred, e.g. Saturday night in a hotel, these must be met by the individual employee.

Travel with a spouse or partner. If a member of staff is accompanied by a spouse or partner who is not involved in Company business, the traveller must bear the cost of their spouse/partner. It is not permitted to downgrade the travel or accommodation booked in order to fund travel costs for a companion. If there is a business reason for a spouse or partner to accompany the Company member of staff, this should be pre-approved in writing by the Finance Director and any additional costs incurred by the Company for the companion will be treated as a benefit-in-kind. Spouses/partners not engaged or employed by the Company are not covered by Company insurance.

Frequent traveller schemes and personal incentives. Membership of a frequent traveller scheme must not deflect from using the most cost-effective option presented by the company's preferred suppliers. The company will not reimburse frequent traveller membership fees.

Group travel. Group travel should be limited to a number that would not critically affect the continuity of Company's operations in the event of an accident. If more than two Company personnel are planning to travel together please contact Company Secretary about insurance cover.

8. Subsistence

Meals. No meals will be reimbursed while you are at the head office, irrespective of whether or not it is your base and whether or not it has catering facilities.

Meals whilst away overnight. When necessarily away from base overnight, the Company will reimburse the actual cost of relevant meals on presentation of receipts, up to the limits (including VAT and service) below:

Meal	Limit (incl. VAT and service)
Breakfast	£5
Lunch	£5
Dinner	£10

Where appropriate, staff may dine in the hotel and claim the actual cost of a reasonable meal. If certain meals have been provided for you, such as breakfast being included in the accommodation charge, only the other meals may be claimed.

Meals where there is no overnight stay involved. When on Company business with no overnight stay you may claim the cost of a meal on production of a receipt, provided all of the following conditions are met: **(1)** you are working away from your normal place of employment for a period expected to exceed five hours; and **(2)** you are working more than five miles away from your normal place of employment or it is not practical for operational reasons for you to return to your workplace.

The receipt for this meal cannot be for food ordered for delivery to your home or purchased elsewhere and consumed at home. The usual rate for such a meal is £5 (including VAT and service). After 8pm, where staff have been on duty for more than five hours, the rate is increased to the higher "dinner" rate of £10 (including VAT and service); this also applies where the meals are eaten/purchased before 8pm, provided duty finishes after 8pm. Details of the qualifying circumstances, must be included on the claim. In addition, where your working day exceeds eleven hours of duty away from your home and all of the above conditions are met, the cost of a second meal can be claimed. The maximum total of the two meals should not usually exceed £20 (including VAT and service).

9. Telephone

Business phone calls. When you use your own home or mobile phone on Company business, the cost of itemised business calls will be met on production of an itemised bill. No rental charges will be paid by the Company, irrespective of whether these include a certain amount of free call time. HMRC will only allow the Company to reimburse the business call costs.

The Company will not meet the cost of phone cards for pay-as-you-go mobiles.

If no itemised bill is available, a schedule of logged business calls should be attached. This will be acceptable provided the total is less than £ .... *(insert figure)* per quarter.

The Company will meet the cost of business calls from a call box or hotel room, provided details of the call, including the length and to whom, are included on the expense claim.

The Company will not reimburse the cost of hands-free equipment or accessories.

10. Entertaining

Business entertainment. The cost of hospitality should be met by the most senior person in attendance and their expense claims must always be authorised by someone who did not attend the hospitality event. The hospitality should be appropriate and never include champagne.

Invoicing the company directly should not be used to settle the cost of business entertaining, even when the cost exceeds £ ……….. *(insert figure)*.

Entertaining business contacts. The Company recognises that it may be necessary to provide hospitality to business contacts from external organisations. You should discuss the business purpose and level of expenditure in advance with your authorising manager. The level should be appropriate and not exceed £ ……….. *(insert figure)* per head (including VAT and service); claims above this level will require authorisation from the Managing Director or Finance Director and will only be granted in exceptional circumstances. The number of company staff should be no more than the number of business contacts. The cost should be met by the most senior person in attendance and claimed back via expenses.

You should be aware that client entertaining may amount to bribery, which is a criminal offence, where the person offering the hospitality intended the recipient to be influenced to act improperly. This is most likely to be the case where the hospitality is excessive or unreasonable. Therefore, all client entertaining expenses will be closely monitored by the Company.

Staff entertainment. Any staff entertaining must be approved in advance. The cost should be met by the most senior person in attendance and claimed back via expenses. The names of those entertained and their staff numbers must be included on the expense claim. The expense claim must always be authorised by someone who did not attend the hospitality. The entertaining should be appropriate and never include champagne. Staff are responsible for the cost of getting to and from such events.

Invoicing the company directly can only be used for staff events costing more than £ ……… *(insert figure)*; the notification of taxable benefit form must be submitted.

Christmas parties and annual events. It is recognised that at certain times of the year a social occasion for all staff to mix informally may be appropriate. It is usual for you to make a contribution towards the cost of such an occasion, but where your contribution does not cover the actual cost, the Company may meet the difference, with the approval of your authorising manager. A cumulative total of costs per person during the tax year is kept, and provided the company's contribution to such annual events is within the limits set by HMRC no tax liability will arise.

Charitable donation. Financial donations to registered charities or community organisations must not be made with company money. Any requests for other forms of support for charities or community organisations, of whatever nature, should be checked and cleared first with the Company's Finance Director. The only circumstances in which payment may be made to charities is where a contributor requests us to do so in lieu of payment for their services.

11. Other expenses

1. Interest and card costs

You are responsible for interest and charges due to late payments of the balance on your credit or charge card. However, if you have submitted a correctly completed expenses claim in sufficient time and payment was subsequently delayed through no fault of your own, causing you to incur interest, you may submit a claim for the relevant charges.

You should not wait for your card statement before submitting your claim.

2. Cash advance handling fee

Company policy requires that, where you need to pay for items in cash, you should withdraw that cash yourself using a Company or your own card. You may claim the cost of the cash advance handling fee charged by the card provider for such an advance. You must attach a copy of the statement to your claim and state on the claim why cash was required.

3. Clothing

It is your responsibility to provide suitable clothing for your normal duties. If exceptionally specialist clothing is required for a one-off event, an authorising manager can agree in advance to reimburse the cost of hiring specialist clothing worn in the performance of your duties. The Company would not expect to pay for the hire of clothing required to attend an award ceremony or similar event.

In accordance with the health and safety regulations, the Company will provide specific employees with the necessary protective clothing or make a contribution towards their purchase. The maximum contribution will be £ .... (insert figure) every three years and the Company must keep a record of those in receipt of the protective clothing allowance.

Protective clothing which could be considered as "ordinary" clothing, such as thermal jackets or waterproofs must have a "Company" logo on each garment or the contribution towards the cost will be reported as a taxable benefit. An original invoice must be attached to the expense claim.

4. Eye tests and glasses

If you use display screen equipment as part of your work for the Company for more than two hours each day, you can apply to your manager for an eyesight test using the health referrals eye tests form. The Company will reimburse the cost of an eyesight test.

Where the eye examination shows that glasses are needed specifically for DSE work, the Company will contribute to the cost. The Company will pay up to £ ……… *(insert figure)* for the basic prescription cost of the lenses and up to £30 for the frames. Your optician must complete the final section on the "eyesight tests" form to indicate that the glasses are specifically required for DSE work.

You should claim the actual cost of the test and, where applicable, glasses, up to the maximum contribution and attach your receipt and the fully completed "eyesight tests" form to your claim.

12. Subscriptions to professional organisations

Professional fees and subscriptions paid by or on behalf of an employee to an organisation, included in HMRC List 3, where the activities of the organisation are relevant to the office of employment in accordance with s.343 and 344 Income tax (Earnings and Pensions Act) 2003, can be claimed for.

The activities of the organisation are relevant to the office or employment if the performance of the duties is directly affected by the knowledge that the organisation exists to provide, or they involve the exercise of the profession that organisation represents.

The Company will meet the cost for an employee to be a member of any professional organisation.

13. Working from home

The Company will not provide for broadband or equipment at home. The only exceptions are if the Company decides that you should be able to work from home either as a homeworker or for business continuity reasons, in which case the use of any equipment provided by the Company must be restricted to business. For these exceptions an authorising manager can agree the provision of business equipment; the Company will not provide such equipment where the member of staff has equivalent equipment in a Company's office building. A record of all equipment provided to you must be maintained by the authorising manager/business manager. All equipment loaned to you remains the property of the Company and must be returned when you leave. Provided this is complied with, it will not result in a taxable benefit.

If the Company considers it necessary as part of these arrangements, it may agree to the installation of a separate business telephone line with broadband service solely for business use. Installation must be arranged by the Company and the Company will pay all charges direct. If instead you decide to install a second telephone line, you can claim only for the cost of business calls supported by an itemised bill. If you decide to install broadband yourself, no costs can be claimed.

If you are a homeworker, you can claim an allowance of £156 per annum towards the cost of light, power and heat; this should be claimed six monthly in arrears.

14. Payments to casuals, freelancers or sub-contractors

No payment can ever be made by an employee of the Company to a casual or a freelancer or a sub-contractor through expenses.

Notes

Notes

Notes

Notes

Notes

Notes

Notes

Notes